Arthur Penrhyn Stanley

Sermons preached before His Royal Highness the Prince of Wales

during his tour in the East, in the Spring of 1862, with notices of some of the localities visited

Arthur Penrhyn Stanley

Sermons preached before His Royal Highness the Prince of Wales
during his tour in the East, in the Spring of 1862, with notices of some of the localities visited

ISBN/EAN: 9783337082840

Printed in Europe, USA, Canada, Australia, Japan

Cover: Foto ©ninafisch / pixelio.de

More available books at **www.hansebooks.com**

SERMONS

PREACHED BEFORE

HIS ROYAL HIGHNESS THE PRINCE OF WALES,

DURING

HIS TOUR IN THE EAST,

IN THE SPRING OF 1862,

WITH NOTICES OF SOME OF THE LOCALITIES VISITED.

By ARTHUR PENRHYN STANLEY, D.D.

REGIUS PROFESSOR OF ECCLESIASTICAL HISTORY IN THE UNIVERSITY OF OXFORD; HONORARY CHAPLAIN IN ORDINARY TO THE QUEEN; DEPUTY CLERK OF THE CLOSET; HONORARY CHAPLAIN TO THE PRINCE OF WALES.

NEW YORK:
CHARLES SCRIBNER, 124 GRAND STREET.
1863.

[*Published by arrangement with the Author.*]

Dedicated

TO

HIS ROYAL HIGHNESS

ALBERT EDWARD, PRINCE OF WALES,

PREFACE.

THE Sermons in this volume are now for the first time given to the public, in deference to the gracious expression of Her Majesty's wishes.

It will be seen that their interest depends entirely on the circumstances and the occasion of their delivery. A more elaborate style, or more copious illustrations, would have been out of place in the original composition of such Addresses, and would, if subsequently added, have destroyed the only value which they possess. Whatever special allusions they may contain to the scenes of the journey will, it is believed, be sufficiently explained in the Notices added at the conclusion of the volume.

These Notices have been written, in compliance with a desire, kindly expressed by His Royal Highness the Prince of Wales, that some record should be left of a journey so interesting not only to those more immediately concerned, but to the public at large.

Any continuous narrative of the Tour was precluded by the circumstances of the case. The mode of travelling was too rapid to admit of scientific investigations. The scenes visited, being of necessity the most famous and familiar of the sacred and classical localities, have been delineated so often, and in such detail, as to render any fresh account superfluous. Of most of them I had myself said all that I could hope to say in a previous work on the history and geography of Palestine.

But there were, notwithstanding, a few scenes which, partly owing to the advantages attendant on His Royal Highness's presence, partly from the occasional novelty of the route pursued, appeared to me deserving of a more special commemoration. The Notices of these localities I have accordingly appended to the Addresses, with which they are connected, if not by way of actual illustration, at least by association of time and place. And, although in substance these descriptions have been or will be incorporated in other works, yet I venture to hope that my fellow-travellers will not be averse to possess, in the same Memorial of our Eastern Tour, reminiscences both of our Sundays and our week-days — of some of the scenes which we explored and enjoyed together, as well as of the more serious thoughts which their sacred recollections suggested.

As the Sermons remain unaltered, so I have left the Dedication to the Prince of Wales in the form in which it was written immediately after our return.

But now, on the eve of the auspicious event which promises so abundantly to fulfil the hopes then expressed for the welfare of His Royal Highness, He will, I trust, graciously accept the offering of this little volume in its new form. It is presented to Him as a pledge of the humble and sincere interest with which a former travelling companion joins the prayers of the whole nation for His lasting happiness, on this solemn step in the great journey of life with Her who will henceforward share the responsibilities, grace the pleasures, and lighten the cares of all its various scenes.

CHRIST CHURCH, OXFORD,
February 27, 1863.

CONTENTS.

SERMONS IN THE EAST.

PAGE

DEDICATION, ... xiii

SERMONS PREACHED IN EGYPT.

SERMON I.

ABRAHAM IN EGYPT, ... On the Nile, 21
Abraham went down into Egypt to sojourn there.
                                                        Gen. xii. 3.

SERMON II.

ISRAEL IN EGYPT, ... At Thebes, 29
Thou hast brought a vine out of Egypt. — *Ps.* lxxx. 8.
I am the Lord thy God, which brought thee out of the land
of Egypt. — *Ps.* lxxxi. 10.

SERMON III.

JOSEPH IN EGYPT, ... On the Nile, 37
Joseph's ten brethren went down to buy corn in Egypt.
                                                        Gen. xlii. 3.

PREACHED IN PALESTINE.

SERMON IV.

THE FRAGMENTS THAT REMAIN, ... At Jaffa, 45
Gather up the fragments that remain, that nothing be lost.
                                                        John vi. 12.

SERMON V.

CHRIST AT JACOB'S WELL, ... At Nablûs, 53
Let this mind be in you, which was also in Christ Jesus.
                                                        Phil. ii. 5.
God is a Spirit: and they that worship Him must worship
Him in spirit and in truth. — *John* iv. 24.

CONTENTS.

SERMON VI.
JESUS OF NAZARETH, ... At Nazareth, 61
(GOOD FRIDAY.)

> Pilate wrote a title and put it on the cross. And the writing was, "Jesus of Nazareth, the King of the Jews." — *John* xix. 19.

SERMON VII.
CHRIST AT THE SEA OF TIBERIAS, ... At Tiberias, 69
(EASTER-DAY.)

> After these things, Jesus showed himself again to the disciples at the sea of Tiberias; and on this wise showed he himself. — *John* xxi. 1.

PREACHED IN SYRIA.

SERMON VIII.
S. PAUL ON THE WAY TO DAMASCUS, ... At Rasheya, 79

> And as he journeyed, he came near Damascus. — *Acts* ix. 3.

SERMON IX.
THE GIFTS OF NATURE, ... At Baalbec, 87

> In them hath he set a tabernacle for the sun, which cometh forth as a bridegroom out of his chamber, and rejoiceth as a giant to run his course. It goeth forth from the uttermost part of the heaven, and runneth about unto the end of it again: and there is nothing hid from the heat thereof. — *Ps.* xix. 5, 6.

SERMON X.
THE LAST ENCAMPMENT, ... At Ehden, 97

> And it came to pass, when the ark set forward, that Moses said, Rise up, Lord, and let thine enemies be scattered; and let them that hate thee flee before thee. And when it rested, he said, Return, O Lord, unto the many thousands of Israel. — *Num.* x. 35, 36.

CONTENTS.

PREACHED ON THE MEDITERRANEAN.

SERMON XI.

S. JOHN AT PATMOS AND AT EPHESUS, ... 109
When He, the Spirit of Truth, is come, He will guide you into all truth. — *John* xvi. 13.

SERMON XII.

S. PAUL IN EUROPE, ... 119
Last of all, He was seen of me also ... that am not meet to be called an apostle.... But by the grace of God I am what I am ... I labored more abundantly than they all, yet not I, but the grace of God which was with me. — 1 *Cor.* xv. 8–10.

SERMON XIII.

THE GIFT OF THE SPIRIT, ... 129
(WHITSUNDAY.)
The Comforter, which is the Holy Spirit, whom the Father will send in my name, He shall teach you all things. Peace I leave with you, my peace I give unto you: not as the world giveth, give I unto you.
John xiv. 26, 27.

PREACHED IN WINDSOR CASTLE.

SERMON XIV.

THE BREADTH OF GOD'S COMMANDMENT, ... 137
(TRINITY SUNDAY.)
I see that all things come to an end, but Thy commandment is exceeding broad. — *Ps.* cxix. 96.

NOTICES OF SOME OF THE LOCALITIES VISITED DURING THE TOUR OF THE PRINCE OF WALES IN THE EAST.

	PAGE
INTRODUCTION,	149

Egypt — Jerusalem.

I. THE MOSQUE OF HEBRON, ... 157
  The Cave of Machpelah.
  The Visit of the Prince of Wales.
  The Tomb of David at Jerusalem.
  Journey to Hebron.
  Entrance into the Mosque.
  The Neighborhood of Hebron.

II. THE SAMARITAN PASSOVER, ... 199
  The Passover on Mount Gerizim.
  The Antiquities of Nablûs.

III. GALILEE, ... 215
  Cana.
  Tabor.
  The Lake of Gennesareth.
  Safed.
  Kedesh-Naphtali.

IV. HERMON AND LEBANON, ... 235
  The Valley of the Litâny.
  The Temples of Hermon.
  Baalbec.
  Damascus.
  Beirût.
  The Cedars of Lebanon.
  Arvad.

V. PATMOS, ... 263
  Its Traditions.
  Its Connection with the Apocalypse.

DEDICATION.

Sir,

You will perhaps remember that, on one of the Sundays of our journey through Palestine, Your Royal Highness was pleased to express a wish that the Sermons which I used to address to our little congregation, should, on our return, be privately printed for their use.

This request is fulfilled in the accompanying volume. It contains the Addresses delivered before Your Royal Highness on every Sunday during our Eastern Tour, with the exception of the three occasions (at Cairo, Jerusalem, and Constantinople) when we fell in with the usual ministrations of the English Church in those places. They are printed almost exactly as they were preached. Their brevity and their abruptness of style is left unaltered. Nor have I attempted to enlarge on the many topics which are too lightly touched; or to omit those which I have treated at length elsewhere. These peculiarities, which must be excused by the circumstances of their composition and delivery, may, at least, have the advantage of recalling more fully to those who heard them the impressive scenes amidst which they were preached.

. . . .

Of those who so heard them, one, whose approval I should have especially valued, has, since these lines were written, been taken from amongst us. This is not the place to speak of the great loss which Your Royal Highness has sustained in the death of your faithful friend and counsellor, General Bruce. But in presenting to you these memorials of a time, with which he must be ever connected in the minds of his fellow-travellers, I may be allowed to dwell for a moment on the thoughts suggested by an association so affecting and so endearing to all those concerned.

In one of the last of our Syrian Sundays, I ventured to express our joint thankfulness*

---

* See Sermon IX.

for the health and happiness which had been granted to us during our late expedition. I have left this expression unchanged; because I know that it represented his feeling at the time, and because I feel sure that he would not have wished his untimely end to have cast an undue shade over the remembrance of a journey, in the success of which he had himself taken so deep an interest, planned as it had been by Him, whose loss clouded with so heavy a sorrow the commencement of our Tour. If other griefs overshadowed its continuance, this last visitation, which was to follow so mournfully on its close, was as yet veiled in the future. We may still be permitted, as we recall many a happy and many a serious hour during those four memorable months, to cherish unbroken the constant image of the noble figure of our beloved and gallant Chief, as he rode at our head, or amongst us, through the hills and valleys of Palestine; or the easy pleasantry with which he entered into the playful moods of our mid-day halts and evening encampments; or the grave and reverential attention with which he assisted at our Sunday Services;

or the tender consideration with which he cared for every member of our party; or the example, which he has left to all, of an unfailing and lofty sense of duty, and of entire devotion to the charge committed to him. These things we can never forget, whenever we think of the days of that Eastern journey, of which the recollection will endure to the end of our lives.

For him it has been ordered otherwise. It was the famous desire of another of his name and race, that the heart of Robert Bruce should be laid in the Holy Land. His remains now repose, not unworthily, beside those of that Royal ancestor. He, in his journey to the Holy Land, gave up his heart and life in the service of his Queen and of his country. He has passed, we trust, into that Holier Land, where he shall rest under the shadow of the perfect Reign of Righteousness and Peace, which on earth he strove with all his might to advance and to secure. If these Discourses — which I now, with a grateful and respectful remembrance of much kindness, dedicate to your Royal Highness — can in any way assist in promoting the good of One whose future is so dear to all of us, and for whose welfare his dying wish was offered up, they will have accomplished the object of their author,

Your obliged and faithful Servant,

ARTHUR PENRHYN STANLEY.

July 3, 1862.

DIRECTIONS TO BINDER.

Sketch Plan of the Mosque at Hebron . . *to face page* 157
Plan of Mount Gerizim . . . . " 199
Plan of the Cedars of Lebanon . . . " 253

SERMONS IN EGYPT.

SERMON I.

ABRAHAM IN EGYPT.

SERMON I.

ABRAHAM IN EGYPT.

PREACHED ON THE NILE, BETWEEN CAIRO AND THEBES, ON THE
FIRST SUNDAY IN LENT, MARCH 9, 1862.

Abraham went down into Egypt to sojourn there. — GEN. xii. 10.

IT may have struck some of us, as it struck me, when the First Lesson of last Sunday afternoon was read at Cairo, containing these words, that it was a fitting welcome to our arrival in this country. It is the earliest mention of that connection of Egypt with the Bible which was never afterwards lost. In those few verses, which describe the visit of Abraham, some of the main features of the country appear, as we see them at this day. The great river was flowing then, as it had flowed for ages before, and has flowed for ages since, scattering verdure and fertility along its banks, so that when Abraham found a famine elsewhere, he could still be sure of finding plenty in Egypt. There was already seated on the Egyptian throne one of the ancient dynasty, called by the name of the Sun, whose brightness and penetrating power we feel so powerfully at this moment, Pharaoh, "the Child or Servant of the Sun." And it is clear from the account that this Pharaoh was not the first of his race; that he was one of a long succession that had gone before. The monarchy had already grown up; his court and his princes were round him, and his power and his fame were so great as to inspire awe and terror into the heart of the simple Shepherd Chief, who came with his wife from Palestine; and when that Shepherd Chief goes away, the Egyptian King lavishes upon him, with a profusion of liberality, all the gifts of Egypt, such as we now see them, and such as would be most acceptable to one who was still a traveller and wanderer in the desert: droves of " oxen and " herds of " sheep, and he-asses and she-asses, and camels."

This is our first introduction to Egypt in the Bible. Let us ask, on this day, what religious lessons it is intended to teach us: what was the relation of Egypt to the Chosen People and the religious history of mankind?

It is, in one word, the introduction of the Chosen People to the *World* — to the world, not in the bad sense in which we often use the word, but in its most general sense, both good and bad.

1. Egypt was to Abraham — to the Jewish people — to the whole course of the Old Testament, what the world, with all its interests and pursuits and enjoyments, is to us. It was the parent of civilization, of art, of learning, of royal power, of vast armies. The very names which we still use for the *paper* on which we write, for the sciences of Medicine and *Chemistry*, are derived from the natural products and from the old religion of Egypt. We might think, perhaps, that the Bible would take no account of such a country — that it would have seemed too much belonging to this earth, and the things of this earth. Not so;

from first to last, this marvellous country, with all its manifold interests, is regarded as the home and the refuge of the chosen race. Hither came Abraham, as the extremest goal of his long travels, from Chaldea southwards; here Joseph ruled, as viceroy; here Jacob and his descendants settled as in their second home, for several generations; here Moses became "learned in all the wisdom of the Egyptians." From the customs and laws and arts of the Egyptians, many of the customs, laws, and arts of the Israelites were borrowed. Here, in the last days of the Bible history, the Holy Family found a refuge. On these scenes, for a moment, even though in unconscious infancy, alone of any Gentile country, the eyes of our Redeemer rested. From the philosophy which flourished at Alexandria came the first philosophy of the Christian Church. This, then, is one main lesson which the Bible teaches us by the stress laid on Egypt. It tells us that we may lawfully use the world and its enjoyments, — that the world is acknowledged by true religion, as well as by our own natural instincts, to be a beautiful, a glorious, and, in this respect, a good and useful world. In it our lot is cast. What was permitted as an innocent refreshment to Abraham; what was enjoined as a sacred duty on Moses and Apollos; what was consecrated by the presence of Christ our Saviour, we too may enjoy and admire and use. Power and learning and civilization and art may all minister now, as they did then, to the advancement of the welfare of man and the glory of God.

2. But, secondly, the meeting of Abraham and Pharaoh, — the contact of Egypt with the Bible, — remind us forcibly that there is something better and

higher even than the most glorious, or the most luxurious, or the most powerful, or the most interesting, sights and scenes of the world, even at its highest pitch, here or elsewhere.

Whose name or history is now best remembered? Is it that of Pharaoh, or of the old Egyptian nation? No. It is the name of the Shepherd, as he must have seemed, who came to seek his fortunes here, as a stranger and sojourner. Much or little as we, or our friends at home, rich or poor, may know or care about Egypt, we all know and care about Abraham. It is his visit, and the visit of his descendants, that gives to Egypt its most universal interest. So it is with the world at large, of which, as I have said, in those old days Egypt was the likeness. Who is it that, when years are gone by, we remember with the purest gratitude and pleasure? Not the learned, or the clever, or the rich, or the powerful, that we may have known in our passage through life; but those who, like Abraham, have had the force of character to prefer the future to the present,—the good of others to their own pleasure. These it is who leave a mark in the world, more really lasting than Pyramid or Temple, because it is a mark that outlasts this life, and will be found in the life to come. He comes into contact with Egypt, with the world; he uses it; he enjoys it. It is but one of the halting-places in his life. He falls for a moment under its darker influences; for a moment he yields to the fear of man, and to the temptation of unworthy deceit. But in the next moment he is himself again. He is what we see him in the chapter which has just been read, describing the offering of Isaac,—willing to sacrifice whatever is nearest and dearest to the call of God and of duty. Heathen traditions represent him as teaching the Egyptians the astronomy that he brought with him from Chaldea; or as reconciling their theological and political disputes. But this is not that for which he is remembered in the Bible and by mankind at large. It is as the Friend of God, and as the Father of the Faithful. It is not for those points which distinguish him from the rest of mankind, but for those points which we may all have in common with him.

His character and his name, as compared with that of the mighty country and the mighty people, in the midst of which we thus for an instant find him, exemplify, in the simplest yet strongest colors, the grand truth that "man shall not live by bread alone, but by every word that proceedeth out of the mouth of God." To be in the world, but not of it; to use it without abusing it, — this is the duty which we find it so hard to follow; but it is the very duty which Abraham first, and our blessed Lord afterwards, have set before us. It is what the hermits and monks, who buried themselves in the caves and tombs of this country, failed to see on the one side; it is what mere men of the world fail to see on the other side. But it is what we may and ought to follow, if, with God's blessing, we strive to walk in the steps of our first father Abraham, of our Lord and Saviour Jesus Christ.

SERMON II.

ISRAEL IN EGYPT.

SERMON II.

ISRAEL IN EGYPT.

PREACHED ON THE SECOND SUNDAY IN LENT, MARCH 16, IN THE GREAT HALL OF THE TEMPLE OF KARNAK AT THEBES.

Thou hast brought a vine out of Egypt. — PSALM lxxx. 8.
I am the Lord thy God, which brought thee out of the land of Egypt.
PSALM lxxxi. 10.

WHEN I spoke last Sunday about Egypt, and its relation to the Bible, I said that there were two sides which it presented: one is, that of contrast to the Chosen People; and the other is that of likeness and sympathy. These two points appear in the Psalms of the day which we have just heard. Let us briefly touch on both as regards not merely the country, but the worship and the religion, of Egypt.

I. The points of likeness.

1. The power of Religion. This it was which gave form and direction to the great works which we see. These buildings are the oldest consecrated places of worship in the world, — older than anything else existing, — older than any Christian Church, — older than the Jewish Temple. From these the leading idea of Solomon's Temple was taken. In them the principles of religious art first appeared, which have never since been lost.

2. The belief in a Future Judgment and a Future Life. This caused the old Egyptians to build their vast tombs, and embalm their bodies, as if to last forever. They were the first nation that had the great and elevating thought of thinking more of the future than of the present, — of the unseen world than the seen.

3. The religious feeling of intense thankfulness for the gifts they enjoyed. Hence the thousands of offerings represented on these walls, as if they could not be thankful enough.

In all these points, we may say, with St. Paul at Athens, "That unknown God whom they thus ignorantly and imperfectly worshipped, Him the true Religion has declared to us since more clearly;" and we may well ask ourselves, as we look round on these rude but gigantic steps towards a better knowledge of God, whether, with that better knowledge of Him, we serve Him with anything like the same devotion and success as that which marked the efforts of those first forefathers of the faith and worship which we have been permitted to enjoy.

II. But the Bible — and especially the account of the time when Israel came out of Egypt — bids us still more to reflect on the change made by the Exodus of the Israelites, for them and for us.

1. It was their *deliverance* from Egypt. Whatever else the Exodus was, it was the first inauguration, the first sanction, of the blessing of freedom and liberty. Every Englishman knows what this is: to be a citizen of a free country, of a free commonwealth, — to have liberty of speech and action and conscience. This is that of which the old world, on which we are now

treading, had no conception. These enormous buildings were raised by the labor of countless slaves. Those countless slaves looked up to the tremendous kings who ruled over them, and in whose presence we now stand, with a feeling of awe and terror of which we can now hardly form any notion. In their day, this awful terror, no doubt, had its use. It was the earliest stage in the education of mankind; to it we owe these astonishing works, which have guided the thoughts of men ever since. But, if the world were ever to make progress, — if the soul of man were ever to be what God intended it to be, — it must be able to walk by itself, to lean upon itself and upon God, and not upon any human power, however great. This is what was effected for Israel, for Christendom, for the whole human race, when God, by the hand of Moses and Aaron, led His people out of the house of bondage and the dominion of Pharaoh. If, in this and other Eastern countries, the freedom which was then given has never yet been fully enjoyed, yet not the less is it our most precious privilege. May we all have grace to act and think and live worthily of that freedom, — that manly freedom, — that glorious liberty of the children of God, wherewith God and Christ have made us free.

2. It is impossible not to feel more strongly here than anywhere else what was the special need and force of the First Commandment, "Thou shalt have none other gods but me." The Unity of God. In the present day we hardly can imagine how any one should have been tempted to think otherwise. But look at the many shapes and figures of the gods to which the wisest nation of the world at that time bowed down.

It may be that even then a few loftier minds saw behind these many forms and shapes One Presiding Spirit. But it was reserved for Moses to make this high truth the inheritance of all classes alike. That *all* should know that there is One and the same God for *all*, — One and the same for rich and poor, for dull and clever, for small and great, this is what the ancient Egyptians hardly could have thought possible. In joy, in sorrow, in the hour of death, and in the day of judgment, whatever else befalls us, and whatever other belief we may have, we all believe, and have endless comfort in the thought, that we are in the hands of One overruling God, who makes all things work together for the best.

3. Still more strongly is the contrast brought out in what we call the Second, but, according to some old divisions, is part of the First Commandment, — "Thou shalt not make to thyself any likeness of anything that is in the heaven above, or in the earth beneath, or in the water under the earth." We cannot doubt that this, to the Israelites, meant that they were not to make to themselves graven images of the hawk and the ibis that fly through the heavens, or the crocodile and the fish that swim in the Nile, or the serpent that creeps in the caves of the earth, or the lion, the jackal, and the wolf, that prowl on the rocky hills. These were the forms under which, at that time of the world, the human mind loved to represent the Divine nature. Perhaps these were the best figures that could be used in those early ages; and we may still learn something from seeing how, out of those earthly shapes, they drew lessons of that which is heavenly and divine. Even to us the animal creation, with all its manifold

instincts and powers, is still, if we rightly reflect, a constant revelation of the Divine mind, of which it is the noble workmanship. But there is a more excellent way of thinking of God, which these imperfect and strange representations shut out from us; and that is, the way which was opened to us, first through Moses, and then through Christ. God is a Spirit; God is Truth; God is Justice; God is Purity; God is Love. Whenever we fancy that He can pass over or be pleased with anything that is untrue, or unjust, or impure, or unlovely, we fall back into worse than the old Egyptian darkness. In proportion as we value and revere truth and justice and purity and loving-kindness, in that proportion we are worthy of the new religion of the new world, to which, by God's grace, we belong.

4. There is the humanity which ran through the law of Israel, and which so rarely appears in the ancient Egyptian religion. The first object that an Egyptian saw, when he came to worship, was the figure of the King receiving the command from the gods to slaughter all his captives. The sons of Israel, on the other hand, were, by the very recollection of their own bondage, entreated to be kind to all those in inferior condition to themselves. In the version of the Ten Commandments in the Book of Deuteronomy this is the reason for observing the rest of the Sabbath. "That thy manservant and thy maidservant may rest as well as thou. And remember that *thou wast a servant in the land of Egypt.*" [1]

No doubt even in the Jewish Law this duty of mercy was very imperfectly recognized. But there were the

[1] Deut. v. 14, 15.

germs of it, of which I have just spoken, — and these were fully developed in the Gospel.

Kindness, consideration to all who come in our way, however different from us in rank, in station, in character, in race, in religion, — this is the doctrine that God through Moses, and, still more entirely, God in Christ, has taught the world; this is the doctrine which even to the great men who left these stupendous monuments was almost unknown. If in vast works like these we are far below them, yet in the little acts of daily love and courtesy and humanity, which are within the reach of all of us, we may, we must be, far above them. . . . .

God grant that when, in days far distant and in places leagues away from hence, we meet in other churches than this, and hear again the same Psalms and the same Commandments read, some of these thoughts may recur to us with fresh force from having been reminded of them here, in the grandest building which the old world ever raised to the glory and worship of God.

SERMON III.
JOSEPH IN EGYPT.

SERMON III.

JOSEPH IN EGYPT.

PREACHED ON THE THIRD SUNDAY IN LENT, MARCH 23, ON THE
NILE, NEAR MEMPHIS.

Joseph's ten brethren went down to buy corn in Egypt. — GEN. xlii. 3.

WITH the story of Joseph, which is now read in the Lessons, we may take farewell of Egypt. It is the fullest account of ancient Egypt that we have in the Bible, and we can now all of us appreciate it better than ever before. We see there Pharaoh, the greatest of earthly kings, surrounded by the officers of his court, just as we see them sculptured on the monuments. We see the green meadow by the riverside, where it is described that the King stood in his dream, and saw the cattle swim up through its waters, and feed on the bank. We see how the Hebrew slave suddenly rises, as in like cases before our own eyes, to be the governor and viceroy of the whole country. We see him invested with the golden chain or necklace, and the royal ring, such as it is still found in the Egyptian tombs. He rides in the royal chariot, such as appears in the processions on the walls of the temples. He is called by an Egyptian name, *Zaphnath-Paaneah*. He marries the daughter of the High Priest of the Hawk-headed God at Heliopolis. He is embalmed with Egyptian skill, and laid out in the usual Egyptian case or coffin. His embalmed body, and that of his father, may still, for all that we know, exist as certainly as those that we have seen preserved unchanged to our own age. There can be no doubt that, as we read the history of Joseph, we are reading the history of one who really lived and died in this country, as surely as any of those whose dead bodies we have handled, or whose actions in their lifetime we have seen, during the last ten days, represented in tombs or temples.

But if the story of Joseph has thus acquired for us a new interest in its outward details, may we not learn again its old familiar lessons with fresh interest also? It is one main characteristic of the Bible, that whilst its letter takes us so very far back from any of the thoughts of our own time and country, its spirit has a value at all times, and in all nations. Let us take two of these lessons.

I. The story of Joseph is a good example of what is meant by Providence working for the best in the lives of men. We find it very difficult, perhaps, to know when we may fairly call any event "Providential" or not. But no one can have lived to the middle period of human existence, and not seem to see in his own life how curiously one part has fitted into the other, which at the time seemed quite unintelligible; how opportunities have been offered, on the acceptance or rejection of which the happiness or the misery of many years afterwards has depended; how sins, which we thought long buried, have started again to our remembrance; how good actions have brought with them a train of blessings, of which at the moment we never dreamed. How like to all this is the story of Joseph! Look at the young foreigner, as he comes to a land not his own; see how he resists the one great temptation of his age and station; observe how, through means not of his seeking, through good report and evil, through much misunderstanding of others, but by constant integrity and just dealing on his own part, he overcomes all the difficulties of his position, and is remembered long afterwards in his adopted land as the benefactor of his generation, and the deliverer of his country. This is the lesson that is first taught us by the history of Joseph, but is repeated, in a measure, through many lands, and in many generations, down to our very nearest experience. Or look at the brothers; how easy it seems to them to remove out of their way the one who embittered their lives, and how, when they could have least expected, they are taunted and tormented and bewildered by the remembrance of the sin of their youth. God was merciful to them; God is merciful to us; but not the less will there come a time, when we shall have our former follies and sins thrown back in our teeth by ourselves or by others: "We are verily guilty concerning our brother, in that we saw the anguish of his soul, when he besought us and we would not hear; therefore is this distress come upon us." "Spake I not unto you, saying, Do not sin against the child, and ye would not hear? therefore, behold, his blood is required." Truly, there is a God that judges the world, and each man in his inmost soul will know it for himself, if not for others. "Divine Justice," it is said in an old proverb, "has leaden feet, but iron hands," — leaden feet that move slowly, but iron hands that make themselves felt at last, whether to strike or to defend, to punish or to reward.

II. There is another lesson from this story of Joseph; indeed, from all this part of the Bible. It is, perhaps, of all the stories in the Old Testament, the one which most carries us back to our childhood, both from the interest which we felt in it as children, and from the true picture of family-life which it presents. How like — how very like — to the incidents of every household is the story of the brothers; of different characters thrown together in the same house, — Judah, Reuben, Simeon, Levi, Joseph, Benjamin, the father, and the mother, Jacob and his lost Rachel! It brings before us the way in which the greatest blessings for this life and the next depend on the keeping up of family-love, pure and fresh, as when the preservation and fitting education of the Chosen People depended on that touching generosity and brotherly affection which no distance of time, no new customs, no long sojourn in a strange land, could extinguish in the heart of Joseph. "Joseph's heart yearned upon his brother." "Joseph could not refrain himself before all them that stood by him, and there stood no man with Joseph when he made himself known unto his brethren. And he wept aloud, and he said, I am Joseph; doth my father yet live?" "And he fell upon his brother Benjamin's neck and wept, and Benjamin wept upon his neck. Moreover, he kissed all his brethren, and wept upon them; and after that, his brethren talked with him."

Surely no long familiar use, no antiquity of Egyptian or Oriental manners, can ever blind us to the deep feeling of that pathetic scene, — of that reunion of all the scattered members of the family in one undivided embrace!

And is not this the very lesson which we all need, and most of all, perhaps, when we are away from our country in a distant land? Many things must be altered as we grow older, and as we change our positions in the world. Many good customs which we retain at home must be altered or suspended when we are abroad. But there are some customs, there are some parts of the human character, which never need be altered, which never ought to be altered, which are best kept up by going back as nearly as possible to the days of our childhood and the thoughts of home. Innocence, — purity of life, — simplicity and truthfulness of character, — regard to our nearest and dearest relations, — daily prayer to God at morning and at evening, — these are amongst the gifts of which our Saviour spoke when he said, " Except ye become as little children, ye shall not inherit the kingdom of heaven." " Of such " childlike characters " is the kingdom of heaven."

HOME, — the scenes, the thoughts, the warnings, the pleasures of home, — the bonds of lasting and cordial affection which reach across seas and continents, and keep us in spirit close to those who in bodily presence are far away, — the images of old days and childlike recollections that visit us in dreams and soothe us in sorrow and calm us in joy, — these are amongst God's best blessings to His creatures, these are amongst the best safeguards He has given us to protect us against new difficulties, strange temptations, corrupting customs. They are the blessings which in different ways we all have in common. Every one of us has a home somewhere, or in some degree, father, or mother, or brother, or sister, or wife, or child. Every one has such an one, far away, it may be, but ever present in thought to us, to whom our well-being is inestimably precious; whose happiness is, or ought to be, inestimably precious to us; to whom no joy is so great as the joy of knowing that we are doing what is right; to whom no grief would be so great as the grief of knowing that we had been doing what was wrong. Of this sacred claim upon us, the Bible constantly reminds us. It reminds us of what this claim is even as regards only this world; but it reminds us also that it is a bond which reaches beyond this world. Those who have passed out of the family circle into the world beyond the grave are, in God's sight, and before our own hearts, still one with us. Whosoever it be that we have so lost (again I repeat each one of those dear and sacred names as they may apply to each of us) — wife, or child, or brother, or sister, or mother, or father — they still call upon us, or rather God calls upon us through them, by what we cherish and honor of them, to remember that their wishes and their hopes for us are not buried in their graves, but will continue as long as their own immortal souls. Their wishes are now commands; their lightest desires now become sacred duties for us who remain. The very mention and thought of their names draws us upward and heavenward. Home is on earth the best likeness of Heaven; and Heaven is that last and best home, in which, when the journey of life is over, Joseph and his brethren, Jacob and his sons, Rachel and her children, shall meet to part no more.

SERMONS IN PALESTINE.

SERMON IV.

THE FRAGMENTS THAT REMAIN.

SERMON IV.

THE FRAGMENTS THAT REMAIN.

PREACHED ON THE FOURTH SUNDAY IN LENT, MARCH 31, ON BOARD
H. M. S. "OSBORNE," IN THE PORT OF JAFFA, BEFORE LANDING
IN PALESTINE.

Gather up the fragments that remain, that nothing be lost. — JOHN vi. 12.

THESE words, from the Gospel of this day, meant, in their first sense, that the disciples were to be careful of the opportunities given them. A miracle had been wrought for their support; but this was no reason why they should expect a succession of miracles. They were to exercise the common duty of forethought, economy, and prudence, and " gather up the fragments that remain, that nothing be lost." Miracles are not wrought without a purpose. God works by the laws of nature; we must do so likewise. Carefulness, order, discipline, — this is the obvious doctrine contained in Christ's command. But the words admit of many other applications.

I. They apply to all marked opportunities. Every dispensation of Providence is a kind of miracle wrought for our benefit. We must make the very most of it. It may be the position in life which is given to us. Every position, great or small, may be made almost as great or as little as we desire to make it, according as we make the most of it or the least of it. To do the necessary duties of any station, that is easy enough; but to gather up all its outlying opportunities; to be ready to lend a helping hand here, to give a kind word there, and a wise counsel there; "to fill," as we say, "our place in life," instead of leaving it half empty; to be entirely in our work for the time being, this is what makes all the difference between a great man and a commonplace man, — a useful man and a useless man, — a good servant and an indifferent servant, — a statesman or teacher, or ruler, who will be long remembered, or one who will be forgotten as soon as he is dead. Or we may have a signal visitation of joy or of sorrow. It is possible to drive such a blessing or such a calamity out of our thoughts, and cut off all its consequences. But it is possible, also, and it is far better, to "gather up all the fragments" that it has left, to see what it has taught us which we knew not before, of our strength, of our weakness; of God, of our own soul. Or it may be that we have known a noble character, a good example. It has gone from us; it is absent from us; we see it no more. Shall we blot out its remembrance? Shall we think that "out of sight is out of mind?" or shall we not rather "gather up all the fragments that remain"—all the sayings, all the doings, all the memories, of such a character, that they may still cheer and sustain, and guide and warn us, in our passage through this mortal life. Or consider our feelings of religion itself. Few and far between, perhaps, may be our prayers and thoughts of serious things; we may find it most difficult to keep them alive (who does not?). But do not despise what you have. One verse from the Bible may be enough to sustain us in sore temptations; one prayer from the Prayer-book may stick to us closer than a brother or a friend; one fixed determination to do what is right may be the rallying-point round which our whole better nature may form and strengthen itself. True, " We are not worthy so much as to gather up the crumbs" of our heavenly Father's table; but " He is the same Lord, whose property is always to have mercy." He blesses, He owns our humblest efforts. For the sake of saving that single spark of good within the soul; for the sake of kindling that smoking flax, and of raising up that broken reed, He sent His Son to this earth, — to this land on which our lot is cast, — to sacrifice Himself for us, in His life and in His death.

II. These thoughts are all brought to a head in considering the country on which we shall this day enter. It is a land, of which the glory has passed away, — of which the interest belongs almost entirely to the past. But it is a land, notwithstanding, of which the name awakens feelings which no other land on the face of this world awakens, — a land in which all have a common interest, — which is known to the humblest cottager in England, as well as to the loftiest in rank or station. How are we to make use of it properly? It is by " gathering up the fragments that remain." There are nothing but fragments. We must not expect grandeur of scenery or splendor of temples; we may, if we choose, " pass through from Dan to Beersheba," and say, " all is barren: there is nothing to be seen." But it is by thinking of what has been here, by making the most of the things we do see in order to bring before our minds the things we do not see, that a visit to the Holy Land becomes a really religious lesson. The heroes and saints of the Old Testament have been here before us. To see the places where they lived and fought and died is not much, but it is something, towards enabling us better to understand and feel what it was for which they so fought and lived and died. The hills and the valleys, and the cornfields, and the birds and the sheep, and the shepherds, and the vineyards, are the very same as those to which the Psalmist, and the Prophets, and our blessed Lord Himself in His parables, made allusions. The Psalms which describe "those who go down to the sea in ships, and do their business in great waters,"[1] the descriptions of the waves of the sea bursting over the rocks,[2] or having "their bounds set that they should not pass,"[3] were suggested by this very harbor of Joppa, in which we now find ourselves. From the vision of S. Peter in the house of Simon the tanner on the seashore at Joppa,[4] went forth the gospel to the Gentile world, till it reached our own distant land. We go up to Jerusalem where Christ died and rose again. To see that Holy City, even though the exact spots of His death and resurrection are unknown, is to give a new force to the sound of the name whenever afterwards we hear it in Church or read it in the Bible.

I do not wish to exaggerate in this matter. It is, thank God, perfectly possible to be just and holy and good, without coming to Palestine. Pilgrimage is not really a Christian duty. Holy places are not really holy in the sight of God, except for the feelings that they produce. The Crusaders were in error, when they thought to save their souls by fighting to regain the Holy Land. It is not the earthly, but the heavenly Jerusalem, which is "the mother of us all," — our

---

[1] Psalm cvii. 23. [2] Psalm xciii. 3, 4.
[3] Jerem. v. 22.   [4] Acts x. 6, 9.

mother in the widest and most endearing sense. But not the less are all these things helps to those who will use them rightly.

When Richard of England first came within view of Jerusalem, he hid his face in his shield, and said, "Ah! Lord God, if I am not thought worthy to win back the Holy Sepulchre, I am not worthy to see it." That is a fine feeling; it is a feeling, at the same time, beyond anything at which we strive to aim. We are not pilgrims: we are not crusaders. But we should not be Christians, — we should not be Englishmen, — we should not, I had almost said, be reasonable beings, if, believing what we do about the events that took place here, we could see Jerusalem and the Holy Land as we would see any other town or any other country. Even if it were only for the thought of the interest which thousands in former ages have taken in what we shall see, — if only for the thought that we shall now be seeing what thousands have longed to see and not seen, — if only for the thought of the feeling which our visit to these spots awakens in the hearts of thousands far away in our own dear homes in England; — we cannot but gather up some good feelings, some more than merely passing pleasure, from these sacred scenes; and can we forbear to add, that there is, besides and above all this, the thought that we may possibly be thus brought more nearly into communion with that Divine Friend and Saviour, whose blessed feet, eighteen hundred years ago, walked this land, through whose words and acts in this country every one of us, at some time of his life or other, has been consoled and instructed, and hopes at last to be saved?

"Gather up the fragments that remain, that nothing

be lost;"—throw away nothing of what we see or hear; throw away nothing of the good recollections and calls to a good life that are still left to us by God's merciful Providence. And, oh, may He gather up, and enable us to gather up, whatever good there is in our hearts and souls! Little enough, He well knows, there is. But whatever that little be,—whatever be the pure intention, or pious feeling, or just thought, or better mind, that remains in each of us,—may He enable us to make the very most of it, here and elsewhere, now and always.

SERMON V.

CHRIST AT JACOB'S WELL.

SERMON V.

CHRIST AT JACOB'S WELL.

PREACHED ON THE SUNDAY BEFORE EASTER, APRIL 13, IN THE
ENCAMPMENT ABOVE NABLÛS (SHECHEM).

Let this mind be in you, which was also in Christ Jesus. — PHILIP. ii. 5.
God is a spirit: and they that worship him must worship him in spirit and
in truth. — JOHN iv. 24.

WE have lately seen much of the contentions between the different Christian Churches in this country. We have seen how vehemently each has contended for its own peculiar possessions, and has thought of nothing else in proportion; how, in consequence of this struggle for what is peculiar to each, that which is common to all has fallen into neglect. This is very like what has gone on in Christendom at large: we have each of us contended for what was peculiar to ourselves, in doctrine, opinions, and customs; we have forgotten that which we have all in common, and which is the most important of all. And what is this? It is, in one word, what the Epistle of this day brings before us, — " The *mind of Christ.*" The *Mind*, the *Character* of Christ, that which He was and is, in that Character which is so wonderfully described to us in the Gospels, — to have this in any degree is what makes a man a Christian; not to have it, is to make all other Christian institutions and opinions almost worse than useless. To enter into the recesses of this Divine Character, more holy than the most revered of earthly shrines; to impress this Mind upon ourselves; to carry away some portion of it home for our daily use, more sacred than the most sacred relics, — this ought to be the object of all that we see as we traverse the scenes of His earthly life; especially, it ought to be my object in what I have to say in these few moments on this Sunday: it is the one main object of that holy ordinance of which, by God's blessing, I trust we may partake on Easter Day.

To dwell on every part of that Character is, within these short limits, impossible. Let me take that which is expressed in the words which I have chosen, as you will all see, because they were spoken close to this very place. By the well which, ages ago, the Patriarch Jacob[1] had, in excess of prudence, dug for his flocks in the noble corn-fields which he had bought for his favorite son Joseph,[2] He, who was passing, as we are, from Judæa[3] through Samaria into Galilee, "sat" in the midday, or the evening, as we might sit, "wearied" by the well. His followers had gone to buy provisions for His meal in the city up the valley; and He sat there, wearied and thirsty and alone, and saw a woman coming to draw water from the well, and made that simple request so natural to all of us, — "Give me to drink." It is one of those touches of fellow-feeling with us which brings Him so near to us, and us to Him, even in bodily presence. It is this moment which is seized in one of the greatest of Christian hymns : —

[1] John iv. 5, 6.   [2] Gen. xxxiii. 19.   [3] John iv. 3.

SERM. V.] *CHRIST BY JACOB'S WELL.* 55

> Quærens me, sedisti lassus;
> Redemisti, crucem passus;
> Tantus labor non sit cassus.
>
> Thou, in search of me, didst sit
> Wearied with the noonday heat;
> Thou, to save my soul, hast borne
> Cross, and grief, and hate, and scorn;
> O, may all that toil and pain
> Not be wholly spent in vain!

The woman who came was a Samaritan — a member of that ancient sect which still lingers on this spot. To her, a stranger, — a heretic, as she was in the eyes of a Jew, — He promised the gift of the water which springs up from no earthly well; the water of life, which rises within the depths of the human soul, and refreshes it with holy thoughts, and good resolutions, and pure feelings, as we pass through this dreary world, bearing each our heavy burden as best we may.

How like to all that He said and did — how unlike, alas! to so much that we say and do. The tender compassion to one who was disliked and despised by His own countrymen, — the boundless toleration of the differences that parted them, — the forbearance towards her hardness and narrowness and incapacity of understanding what He said, — the willingness to enter into a character and a life quite different from His own, — the care and anxiety to do and say something for her good. Which of us is there who does not need some portion of that spirit? — which of us is there who, if he has any portion of that spirit, will not feel rising within himself something of that stream of living water, which shall refresh himself and those around him, and leave a green spot behind, wherever he treads in the hard dry, barren journey of our mortal life.

The conversation proceeds. How exactly it is in conformity with human nature and with Divine wisdom! He reads the secrets of her heart. He touches her own especial fault. She starts aside,— she will not have this mentioned. No. This is just what we all refuse to have touched. We fly, as she did to some general topic: " Sir, I perceive that thou art a prophet." There was the vexed question of doctrine between the Samaritans and the Jews. They worshipped, as they worship still, on Mount Gerizim. To the Jews, Jerusalem was, as it still is, the most holy place. It was out of this question, so naturally suggested by the scenery around Him, that there was brought out that great truth, which has changed the face of religion all over the world. He would not give his decision in favor either of Jews or Samaritans, or, if He did, it was but in passing. ' He would not entangle himself with peculiar doctrines of either of the contending sects. But He gave them what was best for both of them, and is still the best for us. Gerizim and Zion before His prophetic glance melted into one. As he looked out on the wide fields of waving corn which lay before Him, His eye kindled, and His heart swelled (so that " His disciples feared to speak to Him"), and He saw the figure of the new harvest of the world,— of many sects and of many nations, — that was to be gathered in with the fall of the old religion of times and places, and the new spiritual worship, which was to fulfil and embrace the old. " God is a Spirit." Everywhere, at Jerusalem or Gerizim, in Palestine, in England, in church or in chapel, in house or in tent, He accepts the service of his faithful worshippers. And what is that worship? He expresses it in two words, " *Spirit* " and " *Truth.*" " *Spirit* "—We must offer our service, be it short or long, small or great, with a feeling of what we are about,— with a sense of the meaning, of the seriousness, of the awfulness of what we are saying. We must pray with energy, with understanding, with *spirit*. If we have this feeling, then our words, our postures, our acts will become reverential. If not, we shall be still far away from God, however near to Him we may be by His ordinances, by His Church, by outward appearance. " *Truth* "— This is the new grace which Christ has consecrated. " Love of truth, sincerity,"— that our words in prayer shall express what we really want to have granted,— that our lives shall follow in some degree upon our prayers,— that when we call ourselves servants of God, and of Christ, we shall be thinking of doing what is pleasing in His sight, instead of pleasing only our own fancies, or inclinations, or appetites, or ease: this is the true worship which He needs.

We are met together to-day at the beginning of Passion week. We shall be travelling almost every day of it. It is for us to make this week, though travelling, not an unfit celebration of that holy season. The common duties of life, innocent and playful mirth, the act of moving to and fro amongst these beautiful and sacred scenes, these things, I humbly trust, are not inconsistent with the remembrance of Christ's most blessed life and death, if, at the same time (and oh, may God grant that it be so!) our hearts rise to Him in thankfulness, in devotion, "in spirit and in truth, at all such moments as we have to ourselves, in solitary ride or walk, in quiet morning or evening, — to Him, for whom prophet and warrior and ruler and priest of old times all prepared the way, to whom every innocent pleasure, every noble recollection, every lofty wish or thought, is the best offering we can make.

"Christ, our Passover, is sacrificed for us," not with the sacrifice and blood of struggling sheep,[1] and the wild recitations of an ancient ritual, but with that only Sacrifice which is really pleasing to God, — the Sacrifice of a perfect Life and perfect Death. "Therefore let us keep the feast," not with the unleavened cakes or bitter herbs of the Old Dispensation, but " with the unleavened bread of sincerity and truth," transparent, open, conscientious sincerity, and serious, honest, courageous truthfulness, as in the sight of God, who sees our inmost thoughts.

[1] The Samaritan Passover had been thus celebrated on the previous day.

SERMON VI.

JESUS OF NAZARETH.

(GOOD FRIDAY.)

SERMON VI.

JESUS OF NAZARETH.

PREACHED ON GOOD FRIDAY, APRIL 18, IN THE ENCAMPMENT BY
THE SPRING OF NAZARETH.

Pilate wrote a title, and put it on the cross. And the writing was, "Jesus of Nazareth, the King of the Jews." — JOHN xix. 19.

WHAT are the lessons of Good Friday? especially of Good Friday in Palestine and in this place? In the words of the text, in the title written on the Cross, the name of Jesus Christ is at that supreme moment of His Last Passion brought together with the recollection of His early years at Nazareth. What are the lessons which they both teach in common?

I. Everywhere the event of Good Friday speaks to us of the universal love of God to His creatures. That is why it is so truly called *Good* Friday. It has its good news as much as Christmas Day or Easter Day. It tells us not only that God is Love, but that He bears love to every one on this earth, however far they may seem to be removed from Him. It was for this that He sent His Son into the world, — it was for this that Christ died. It was by His death, more even than by His life, that He showed how His sympathy extended far beyond His own nation, His own friends, His own family. "I, if I be lifted up" on the Cross, "will draw all men unto me." It is this which the Collects of this day bring before us. They speak, in fact, of hardly anything else. They tell us how He died that "all estates," not one estate only, but "*all* estates in His Holy Church," — that "*every* member of the Church" in its widest sense, not the clergy or the religious only, but every one, in his "several vocation and ministry," might "truly and godly serve Him." They pray for God's mercy to visit not Christians merely, but all religions, however separate from ours, — "Jews, Turks, Heretics, and Infidels," — in the hope that they may all at last, here or hereafter, be "one fold under one shepherd," the One Good Shepherd who laid down His life not for the flock of one single fold only, but for the countless sheep scattered on the hills, not of the fold of the Jewish people, or of the Christian Church only, but of all mankind.

This is a truth which comes home to us with peculiar force in Palestine. What is it that has made this small country so famous? What is it that has carried the names of Jerusalem and of Nazareth to the uttermost parts of the earth? It is in one word, "the death of Christ." Had He not died as He did, His religion, — His name, — His country, — the places of His birth and education and life, — would never have broken through all the bonds of time and place as they have. That we are here at all on this day, is a proof of the effect which His death has had even on the outward fortunes of the world.

This universal love of God in Christ's death is specially impressed upon us in Nazareth. What Christ was in His death, He was in His life. What He was in His life, He was in His death. And if we wish to know the spirit which pervades both, we cannot do so better than by seeing what we may call the text of His first sermon at Nazareth. He was in the synagogue.[1] The roll of the Hebrew Scriptures was handed to Him. He unrolled it. His former friends and acquaintance fixed their eyes upon Him to see what He would say. And what were the words which He chose? They were these:—" The Spirit of the Lord is upon me, because he hath anointed me to preach the Gospel to the poor; he hath sent me to heal the broken-hearted, to preach deliverance to the captives, and recovering of sight to the blind, to set at liberty them that are bruised, to preach the acceptable year of the Lord." What He said on this text is not described; we are only told that they "marvelled at the gracious words that proceeded out of His mouth." But what those gracious words were we can well see from the words of the passage itself. "The Spirit of the Lord was upon Him," first, "to preach the gospel to the poor," the glad tidings of God's love to the poor, the humble classes, the neglected classes, the dangerous classes, the friendless, the oppressed, the unthought-for, the uncared-for. The Spirit of God was upon Him, secondly, " to heal the broken-hearted:"— to heal, as a good physician heals, not with one medicine, but with all the various medicines and remedies which Infinite Wisdom possesses, all the fractures and diseases and infirmities of our poor human hearts. There is not a weakness, there is not a sorrow, there is not a grievance, for which the love of God, as seen in the life and death of Christ, does not offer some remedy. He has not overlooked us. He is with us. He re-

[1] Luke iv. 18.

members us. The Spirit of God was upon Him, thirdly, "to preach deliverance to the captive." Whatever be the evil habit, or the inveterate prejudice, or the master passion, or the long indulgence, which weighs upon us like a bondage, He feels for us, and will do His utmost to set us free, — to set at liberty those that are cramped and bruised and confined by the chain of their sins, their weakness, their misfortunes, their condition in life, their difficulties, their responsibilities, their want of responsibilities, their employments, their want of employments. And, fourthly, "The Spirit of God was upon Him," to "give sight to the blind." How few of us there are who know our own failings, who see into our own hearts, who know what is really good for us! That is the knowledge which the thought of Christ's death is likely to give us. That is the truth which, above all other truths, is likely to set us free. "Lord, that I may receive my sight," is the prayer which each of us may offer up for our spiritual state, as the poor man whom He met at Jericho did for his bodily eyesight.

For every one of these conditions He died. Not for those only who are professedly religious, but for those who are the least so, — to them the message of Good Friday and of Nazareth is especially addressed. Christianity is, one may almost say, the only religion, of which the Teacher addressed Himself, not to the religious, not to the ecclesiastical, not to the learned world, but to the irreligious, or the non-religious, to those who thought little of themselves and were thought little of by others, to the careless, to the thoughtless, to the rough publican, to the wild prodigal, to the heretical Samaritan, to the heathen soldier, to the thankless peasants of Nazareth, to the swarming populations of Galilee. He addresses Himself, now, to each of us, however lowly we may be in our own eyes, however little we think that we have a religious call, however encompassed we are with infirmities; His love is ready to receive, to encourage, to cherish, to save us.

II. I pass to the other lesson which Good Friday teaches us here. It is that, whatever good is to be done in the world, even though it is God Himself who does it, cannot be done without an effort, — a preparation, — a Sacrifice. So it was especially in the death of Christ, — so it was in His whole life. His whole life from the time when He grew up, "as a tender plant" in the seclusion of this valley, to the hour when He died at Jerusalem, was one long effort, — one long struggle against misunderstanding, opposition, scorn, hatred, hardship, pain. He had doubtless His happier and gentler hours, we must not forget them: His friends at Bethany, His apostles who hung upon His lips, His mother who followed Him in thought and mind wherever He went. But here, amongst His own people, He met with angry opposition and jealousy. He had to bear the hardships of toil and labor, like any other Nazarene artisan. He had here, by a silent preparation of thirty years, to make Himself ready for the work which lay before Him. He had to endure the heat and the cold, the burning sun and the stormy rain, of these hills and valleys. "The foxes" of the plain of Esdraelon "have holes," "the birds" of the Galilean forests "have their nests," but "He had" often "not where to lay His head." And in Jerusalem, though there were momentary bursts of enthusiasm in His behalf, yet He came so directly across the interests, the fears, the pleasures, and the prejudices of those who there ruled and taught, that at last it cost him his life. By no less a sacrifice could the world be redeemed, by no less a struggle could His work be finished.

In that work, in one sense, none but He can take part. "He trod the winepress alone." But in another sense, often urged upon us in the Bible, we must all take part in it, if we would wish to do good to ourselves or to others. We cannot improve ourselves, we cannot assist others, we cannot do our duty in the world, except by exertion, except by unpopularity, except with annoyance, except with care and difficulty. We must, each of us, bear our Cross with Him. When we bear it, it is lightened by thinking of Him. When we bear it, each day makes it easier to us. Once the name of "Christian," of "Nazarene," was an offence in the eyes of the world; now, it is a glory. But we cannot have the glory without the labor which it involves. To "hear His words, and to *do* them," to hear of His death, and to *follow* in the path of His sufferings, this, and this only, as He himself has told us, is to build our house, the house of our life, of our faith, of our happiness, upon a *rock;* a rock which will grow firmer and stronger the more we build upon it, and the more we have to bear. "The rains may descend, and the floods may come, and the winds may blow and may beat upon that house;" but the house will not fall, "for it will have been founded upon the rock."[1]

---

[1] Matthew vii. 25. A storm like that described in this passage was raging throughout Syria on the day when this sermon was preached.

SERMON VII.

CHRIST AT THE SEA OF TIBERIAS.

(EASTER DAY.)

SERMON VII.

CHRIST AT THE SEA OF TIBERIAS.

PREACHED ON EASTER DAY, APRIL 20, BEFORE THE HOLY COM-
MUNION, IN THE ENCAMPMENT BY TIBERIAS.

After these things Jesus showed himself again to the disciples at the sea of
Tiberias; and on this wise showed he himself. — JOHN xxi. 1.

SO S. John, in the last chapter of his Gospel, records the last recollections of his Lord's appearances after the Resurrection. On this, the only Easter Day that in all probability we shall any of us pass on the shores of the Sea of Tiberias, it seems the best use we can make of the occasion, to draw forth all the truth (and it is of various kinds) that this chapter yields in connection with this, the greatest day of the Christian year, with this, the holiest ordinance of the Christian Church.

1. It was after the Lord had risen again that this appearance took place. "The disciples had returned to 'their own homes,' and engaged in their usual occupations; Peter and James and John were again, as they had been before in years past, in their two boats on the lake, throwing in nets to catch the fish which swarm in its waters. Four of their friends were with them,— two whose names are not recorded;

the other two, Thomas, known as the Twin Brother, and Nathanael, from the village of Cana of Galilee. They were once more at their common work. The morning had just broken over the dark eastern hills. The sun shone on the lake and on the tops of the western mountains. On the shore of the sea, — we know not the exact spot, but somewhere along the shelving beach, — there stood a Figure, which arrested their attention. They gazed, but knew not who it was. They heard a voice calling to them, "Children, have ye any food?" They obeyed the advice of the unknown stranger; and then came the rush of fishes into the net, which at once recalled to the disciple who knew his Master best the like scene on the same waters three years before : "The disciple whom Jesus loved turned to Peter and said, ' It is the Lord.' "

Let me pause for a moment to call to mind how like this is to what occurs in human life. These appearances of Christ after His Resurrection seem to be told to us as intimations of what still continues in our relations towards Him : "He is not here, He is risen." He even then had ceased to be to His disciples as He had been before. He went and came suddenly, hardly known by them at first; then known by some gesture, some word, some old association. Is it not so with us? We, like the Apostles, are engaged in our common occupations. We hear a voice from the distance. At first it seems to us only some event or incident of our ordinary life. Suddenly we see, we hear in it the call of Christ, the call of God Himself, calling us to higher thoughts. A familiar recollection of old days sweeps across us, to impress it more firmly upon us; and even in our engagements, our amusements, our fisheries, we recognize the hand, the voice of our merciful Saviour, and are able to say, " It is the Lord."

2. The story goes on. There was a yet closer interview, — a yet nearer sense of that Divine Presence to be brought home to them. We can imagine still more clearly what follows. Peter, who, like the boatmen of these Eastern countries, had thrown off his clothes, to drag up the heavy net, now girded on his fisher's coat, and, with his usual ardor, sprang into the water before the others, and waded up the sloping side of the shore. The rest, in the little boat attached to their larger vessel, came after him; and on the shore they found the meal already spread, and their Lord inviting them to come and partake of it. They felt that it was no common meal; they were struck with awe, — none of them ventured even to say, " Who art thou?" They gathered round him in reverent silence; and " Jesus," we are told, " cometh and taketh bread and giveth them, and fish likewise."

It is impossible, as we read this, not to see the likeness of that holy ordinance of which we this morning partake. It was not, indeed, in form the same, but in spirit it certainly was; and so it was understood in the earliest times. Some of the oldest pictures in the Roman Catacombs represent the Holy Communion under this very figure, — not the twelve disciples, but these seven, with the thin round loaves as of Arab bread, and the fishes lying beside them as from this sacred lake. It is the fitting likeness of the Holy Communion, because it was a meal of the common elements of sustenance, and yet invested with such a solemn and mysterious character, that they who partook of it then felt, as we who partake of it now feel, that there is something in it which brings us nearer than any other ordinance or ceremony of religion into the presence of our Divine Saviour, who is no longer on earth, but in Heaven. It recalled to them, as it recalls to us, the days when He ate and drank and lived with them on earth. It drew their thoughts, as it ought to draw ours, heavenward, to Him who dwells above all our earthly cares and griefs and joys. It drew their thoughts, as it ought to draw ours, to a nearer and closer communion with each other, — with their and our fellow-disciples elsewhere. They must have felt that in that sacred Presence, at least for the time, one only thought was in all their minds alike. We, in like manner, feel, as we partake of this blessed remembrance of His Death and Resurrection, that, however various our characters and stations, one thought for the moment binds us all together, and not us only,— the small company who are here assembled, — but all who are near and dear to us far away; far away in the several homes of our native land; those, too, who are far away in their Eternal Home, and who share in a yet deeper and fuller communion with Him in whose immediate presence they are.

3. And this brings me to the close of the narrative. There were, as I have said, seven only out of the twelve disciples. But these seven contained very different characters, characters so different from each other, as to represent almost every phase of the human soul and mind that can be brought into communion with God and Christ. There was the ardent, impatient, active Peter. There was the devoted, loving John. There was James, the zealous Son of Thunder, the courageous youth who, first of the Apostles, died a

martyr's death. There was Nathanael, the blameless, sincere, and candid Israelite in whom there was to be found no guile. There was Thomas, the doubting, reasoning, inquiring, philosophic Apostle, who believed, in spite of his doubts and because of his reasonable convictions. Each of these, as each of us, stood, or sat, or knelt beside their Master, to receive whatever message He had to give. Of these, two only are specially named, as receiving special warnings or encouragements. But in these two we may all find ourselves included. One was Peter. We need not now think of Peter's peculiar character. We need only remember that he was, as we are, compassed with weakness, — that he had thrice from weakness, as we not thrice only, but many times over, denied his Lord, failed in the hour of trial, done what he most hated himself for having done, left undone that which of all things in the world he would most have desired to have done. To him, as to each of us, in that sacred communion by the sea of Tiberias, our Lord approached, calling him by his own peculiar name and address: " *Simon, son of Jonas, lovest thou Me?* " Thrice, as if for the three denials, He asked this question, as if to show that for all our failings and misdoings in the past there is but one remedy for the future, and that is, to overcome past evil by future good, to blot out fresh failures by renewed exertions in the love and service of goodness. "*Lovest thou Me more than these?*" Yes, that is the great question, — " Lovest thou me ? " " Hast thou any regard for the commands, for the mind, for the spirit of Christ, more than others, above all earthly desires ? " " Hast thou this in any degree ? " We answer, I am sure we should all wish to answer, as he did,

—"*Lord, thou knowest that I love thee.*" "Thou knowest that I wish to love Thee. Thou knowest that here, on this day and in this sacred ordinance, I pledge myself to be Thy disciple. Thou knowest all things; Thou knowest our infirmities; Thou knowest our ignorance; Thou knowest that this is our firm intention and resolution."

So Peter said; so we say and feel also. And to Peter, and to each of us, the same answer comes back as the last charge of our departing Lord, — as the only test of our sincerity in this profession, "*Feed my sheep, Feed My lambs.*" That is, our love to Christ can only be shown by the care, the tender, active, constant care, for the welfare of others, — of those whom He by His Providence has placed or will place in any degree under our charge. To be shepherds of mankind, — this, in its full sense, belongs to the rulers of nations and the pastors of human souls; but, in a lesser sense, it belongs to every one of us who has any influence over those who are near us. To feed, to guide, to support, to be attentive, considerate, kind, helpful, to these, is indeed the best proof of our love of Christ. And this, He continues to say, we must do, even although it cost us much. "*Verily I say unto thee, When thou wast young*, when thou wast a fisherman's boy, on the shores of the Galilean lake, *thou girdedst thyself*, in thy fisher's coat, *and walkedst* over these hills and valleys *whither thou wouldest: but when thou shalt be old*, as years and duties and infirmities increase, *thou shalt stretch forth thy hands*, even on the cross of martyrdom, *and another*, the Roman executioner, *shall gird thee*, with the bonds of imprisonment, *and carry thee whither thou wouldest not*, even to the place where thou must glorify God by thy death." Even so, in speaking to us, He bids us look forward far into the future. We shall not be always as we are now. To most of us, our cares, our difficulties, our restraints, our responsibilities, perhaps our pains and sorrows, will increase. There is but one thing which will turn this bondage into liberty, and that is the final charge which our Lord gives to Peter, "*Follow thou me.*" "Follow thou Christ, in His truth, His justice, His purity, His love, through good report and evil, through joy and grief, through youth and age, and thou wilt never repent of having made that good choice, and chosen that better part."

4. One more word, to guide our thoughts in regard to another kind of character, the Beloved Disciple has left from that parting scene at the Sea of Tiberias. Peter turned, as they walked along the shore, and saw that beloved disciple himself, his own dear friend and companion, following close behind. He longed to know something more of the future fate, something more of the present duty, of that best and bravest and holiest of all the disciples, in comparison with whom he felt himself to be as nothing. He asked, "*Lord, and what shall this man do?*" So we ask concerning those whom we feel to be better and wiser than we, concerning those whom we know to be far above our reach, concerning those whom God has taken to Himself. Where are they? What will be, what is, their fate? What are we, compared with them? Can we ever attain to them? The answer of our Lord to Peter is still the answer to us: "*If I will that he tarry till I come, what is that to thee? follow thou Me.*" It is as though He said, "Trust in Me. My

will and God's will is the best for him and for thee. Leave to me the disposal even of the best and dearest friends thou hast. Vex not thyself with the difference between thyself and them. One duty, one blessing, one happiness, is still left to thee. Though all else be taken away, though their paths and thine be far removed and henceforth asunder, though it seems impossible for us to be as they were and as they are,— Follow thou thy Lord and Master." Follow after Him, though it may be at an immeasurable distance. Follow Him in His long endurance and His great humility. Follow Him in the good deeds which He wrought beside this blessed lake. Follow Him with a bold and cheerful spirit in the happy and glorious victory which He won over sin and over death; and in the end thou shalt find in Him the true communion and fellowship which He only can give, with all who,—far and near, on this side the grave or beyond it,—have cheered and encouraged and urged our affections, forwards, onwards, upwards, from things on earth to things above, where Christ sitteth at the right hand of God.

SERMONS IN SYRIA.

SERMON VIII.

S. PAUL ON THE WAY TO DAMASCUS.

SERMON VIII.

S. PAUL ON THE WAY TO DAMASCUS.

PREACHED IN THE ENCAMPMENT, ON THE ANTI-LEBANON, ON THE FIRST SUNDAY AFTER EASTER, APRIL 27, THE DAY BEFORE REACHING DAMASCUS.

And as he journeyed, he came near Damascus. — ACTS ix. 3.

OF how many travellers has this been said, as of us! How many thoughts have been awakened by the approach to the most ancient of existing cities! Abraham, as he journeyed from the far East, drew near to Damascus, and there halted on his way to the land which was to be his own and his children's for ages to come; and, as it would seem, conquered the great city, already the glory of the East, already the prize of the powerful ones of the earth. Elisha, as he journeyed from Samaria, drew near to Damascus, and met on the road the long train of forty camels, with presents of every good thing of Damascus, to propitiate his favor to the King of Syria, who felt the awe which the coming of the man of God spread before him. Ahaz " went up to Damascus" to meet the great King of Assyria, and there saw the altar so curiously wrought by Syrian art as to become the model of the high altar of Jerusalem. Mahomet, the Prophet of the Mussulman religion, according to the traditions of his own countrymen, as he journeyed from Arabia, drew near to Damascus, and, as he looked down upon the splendid view which we, I trust, shall see to-morrow, said, with a nobleness of sentiment which we cannot but admire, though in another creed than our own, "Man can have but one Paradise in life, — my Paradise is fixed above;" and turned away without entering that glorious city, lest it should tempt him from his prophetic mission. But of all the travellers who, "as they journeyed came near to Damascus," there is none who has such an interest for us as the great Apostle of whom the Second Lesson to-day has spoken to us, and whose path, for the first time in our travels, we thus encounter.

1. Very briefly to-day let us consider his conversion and his preaching. He was on his way from Jerusalem. He "came near Damascus," — we know not how near, we know not by which approach. It was noon; the Syrian sun was bright in the heavens; he was charged with a mission, which admitted of no delay in his eyes, — that of destroying the Christians in Damascus, with a savage zeal like to that which in our own days has laid waste the same city. In one moment, his career was arrested by the heavenly vision which ended in the great act which we call his "conversion." It is an instance, such as we find still occurring but rarely, of a sudden conversion. Yet "a conversion," that is, "a turning round" from bad to good, from good to better, is necessary for us all. We are sometimes inclined to think that our characters, once formed, can never be changed. This is not true; at least it is only half true. Our natural dispositions, our natural faculties, these do very rarely change; but the

direction that they take can be changed; and the difference between their upward and their downward direction is the difference effected by anything which deserves the name of conversion, whether sudden, as in the case of S. Paul, or gradual, as with most of us. He, in great measure, remained the same as he was before, — he retained his zeal, his power, his energy; but the turn which was given to these natural qualities, by his conversion on the road to Damascus, gave a turn to his whole life, and, through him, a turn to the life of the whole world. He approached Damascus, a furious persecutor; he entered it, a humble penitent; he left it, a great Apostle. So is it with us. Much about us never will be changed, never need be changed, never can be changed; but much about us can be changed, ought to be changed, and, with God's good help, will be changed. We are all on the road, not to Damascus only, but to some end or object of our pursuits. To every one of us, as to S. Paul, that end or object will at last appear in a light totally different from what we now expect; and on that changed light may depend our exceeding happiness or our exceeding misery, our great usefulness or our utter uselessness in life.

2. This was the conversion of the Apostle; let us see how it was brought about. It was brought about, first, by the vision of Christ. How this entered into his soul we know not; but that it did enter there, is sure from all that he afterwards did and said. And it is this same communion with Christ, with the goodness, the wisdom, the love of Christ, which still is the most powerful instrument of making every human soul better and wiser and nobler than it was before. It

was, secondly, by calling to his mind the true knowledge of what he was doing. He thought that he was doing God service by trampling down a noxious and heretical sect. That voice from heaven told him that in those poor Christians he was trampling down and persecuting the Great Friend and Deliverer of the world. "*Saul, Saul, why persecutest thou me? I am Jesus whom thou persecutest.*" Yes, so it is still; often and often we think that we are all right; that no one can find fault with us; that those whom we neglect or despise, or set aside, are not worth considering for a moment. And yet all the while, as God sees us, as others see us, we are injuring the very cause we wish to promote; those of whom we think so little may be the very likenesses and representatives to us of God and Christ Himself. In injuring them, in despising them, we may be doing the most wide-spread mischief, we may be defying God, we may be even destroying our own souls. In helping them, in considering them, we are serving Christ Himself. "Inasmuch as ye have done it unto the least of these My brethren, ye have done it unto Me." His conversion was, thirdly, by the appeal to the best part of his own heart. "*It is hard for thee to kick against the pricks,*" against the goad, against the stings, of conscience. He had doubtless already had better feelings stirring within him from what he had seen of the death of Stephen and of the good deeds of the early Christians. In this way his conversion, sudden as it seemed at last, had been long prepared. His conscience had been ill at ease with itself; and in this perplexity and doubt, it needed only that one blessed interposition of his merciful Lord, to recall him to a sense of his better self. Wide as are

SERM. VIII.] *PAUL JOURNEYING TO DAMASCUS.* 83

the differences between us and the Apostle, yet here is a point which we all have in common with him. We each of us have a conscience; each of us has that within him which can be reached, if only we knew how; each of us has a barrier against sin set up within him, against which we may kick and struggle, but which will, thanks to the mercy of God who has placed it there, long resist our efforts. We have but to think of what in our best moments we condemn; that is what we have to avoid; we have but to think of what in our best moments we approve in others; that is what we have to strive for. The recollection of Stephen's martyrdom was probably the first seed of S. Paul's conversion; the recollection of any good act, which has called forth our admiration in past times, may be the beginning of our doing the like in times to come, far beyond anything that we now think or dream of.

3. There is one more thought suggested by S. Paul's conversion on his road to Damascus, and that is what resulted from it. This is too great a subject to be spoken of here in all its parts. But one single point is put before us by the lesson [1] of this morning's Service. What he taught in his Epistles concerns the Church at large; but what he preached to Felix, though it may have concerned especially that unjust and licentious Roman governor, does also in its measure concern each of us as individuals. He "reasoned" with Felix, he argued, he urged, not preaching, not teaching, but talking with him, as one friend eagerly and seriously talks to convince another, on three subjects, on three words, each of which is a

[1] Acts xxiv. 25.

sermon in itself, *Righteousness*, *Temperance*, and *Judgment to come*. *Righteousness*, that is, justice, fairness, impartiality, the duty of dealing calmly and candidly and uprightly with those who are under us, or above us, or equal to us. *Temperance*, that is, self-control, self-restraint, the duty of gaining the mastery over our passions, over our tempers, over our tongues, over our indolence, over our impatience, over our prejudices. *Judgment to come*, that is, the certainty that for everything which we do in this life we shall, sooner or later, have to give an account, and that we shall be judged accordingly by One who knows all our actions, whether public or private, secret or open. When the Apostle spoke of those three things, "Felix trembled;" had we heard him speak, we should have trembled also. Felix trembled for the moment, but he put him off to "a more convenient season." If we wish to make our belief in S. Paul's conversion and the importance of S. Paul's doctrine anything more than a mere name, we shall try to bear away from the road on which it took place the thought of at least these three things, the duty of *justice*, the duty of *self-restraint*, and the certainty of a *judgment to come*.

SERMON IX.

THE GIFTS OF NATURE.

SERMON IX.

THE GIFTS OF NATURE.

PREACHED IN THE ENCAMPMENT UNDER THE TEMPLE OF BAALBEC,
ON MAY 4, THE SECOND SUNDAY AFTER EASTER.

In them hath he set a tabernacle for the sun, which cometh forth as a bridegroom out of his chamber, and rejoiceth as a giant to run his course. It goeth forth from the uttermost part of the heaven, and runneth about unto the end of it again: and there is nothing hid from the heat thereof. — PSALM xix. 4–6

THERE was once a time, in the history of the world, when it was the strongest possible temptation to mankind to worship the great objects of nature, but especially those in heaven, and of these especially the Sun. In these countries more particularly, where the Sun is so bright, so powerful, so omnipresent throughout the year, the temptation was stronger than anywhere else. Wherever in the Old Testament we hear of the worship of Baal, it is the worship of the Sun; and of all the temples so dedicated, this is the most splendid; and the ancient city was called from this worship "Baalbec," or "the City of the Sun." We know from the Bible, we know also from the history of this very Temple, that this worship was corrupted into the most shameful sensuality; so that, to the Israelites first, and to Christians afterwards, it became a duty to put it down altogether. And this corruption is in itself instructive, as teaching us that the highest love of art and the keenest appreciation of what is beautiful, if left to itself, without some purer and higher principles, may and will degenerate into mere brutal self-indulgence and cruelty. But it is always better, if we can, to see what was the good element which lies at the bottom of any character or institution, — what there was in the thoughts that raised these solid foundations and these towering columns, which we also may imitate for ourselves, without falling into those dark errors and sins with which they were once connected.

For this purpose, we could hardly find a more fitting text than the Psalm read in this morning's Service. *"In them hath he set a tabernacle for the sun, which cometh forth as a bridegroom out of his chamber, and rejoiceth as a giant to run his course. It goeth forth from the uttermost part of the heaven, and runneth about unto the end of it again: and there is nothing hid from the heat thereof."* These words, so expressive of the genial life-giving power of the great Light of day, — of the glory of his rising, — of the strength of his rays, — of the regularity of his course, — of the penetrating force of his heat, — spring from a feeling common to the Hebrew Psalmist and to those who raised this heathen Temple. But what are the points wherein they diverge from each other? — or rather what were the good points in that ancient belief, which the True Religion has adopted for its own, and sifted from the surrounding evil? This Temple itself is connected with the history and traditions both of the wisest and greatest thoughts of ancient times, and with the basest and most foolish. Its earliest foundations are said to go back to the days of Solomon, the wisest of men. In its latest times it had for its High Priest the most infamous and effeminate of all the Roman Emperors, — the miserable Heliogabalus. Between the two there was at first sight but little in common. Little, indeed, there is; but it is that little which it is so useful to remember. What then, I repeat, are the points in connection with the reverence for the Sun and for the works of nature, which this Psalm brings before us?

I. There are two points especially, — one at the beginning, the other at the end of the Psalm. The first is a deep sense of thankfulness for those gifts of Nature, as the heathens thought them, of God, as we know them to be. "*The heavens declare the glory of God; and the firmament sheweth his handy-work. Day unto day uttereth speech, and night unto night sheweth knowledge. There is no speech nor language where their voice is not heard. Their line is gone out through all the earth, and their words to the end of the world.*" So the Psalmist spoke; and so we may still feel. Those glorious gifts, which we all enjoy, but never more than when we are travelling, — the delight of a beautiful day, — the lights and shades of sunrise and sunset, — the warmth and brightness which succeed to rain and storm, — the starlit and the moonlit night, — the sight of mountains and rushing streams, — all these may still be to us, as to the Jewish Psalmist, a source not merely of most innocent pleasure, but of religious thankfulness to their Almighty Giver. In the words I have just read, the Psalmist tells of the voice which speaks in these dumb glories of Creation. That voice is surely one which speaks to us with double force now. Now, if ever, we are bound to lift up our hearts in gratitude to the Giver of all good things. For five weeks we have been enjoying His natural gifts of beautiful scenes and glorious weather, and, above all, that inestimable gift of health, of which we think so little till we lose it. One only of our large number has been struck with serious illness, and he has been mercifully restored to us. Let us all join, as we now approach the end of our journey, in a humble and hearty thanksgiving to Him who has thus given us all things freely to enjoy. Those who lived in old time expressed, as we see, their gratitude and reverence for the gifts of nature by this magnificent Temple. Let us express our gratitude and reverence in the offering of pure hearts and good lives to Him who has thus graciously guided us so nearly to the close of our pilgrimage.

II. And this brings me to the second truth which the contemplation of the natural world, — of the sun in his strength, — of the stars as they move in the heavens, — suggested to the Psalmist. He could not look at them without thinking of that characteristic of the works of Creation, which modern science has more and more strongly brought out; the order, the regularity, the *law* of their operations. And this Law immediately recalled his mind to the highest example of all law, — the unchangeable moral Law of God. A great modern philosopher has put the two subjects together in the same connection, probably without thinking that he had been anticipated by the Psalmist of old. "There are two things of which it may be said that, the more we think of them, the more they fill the soul with awe and wonder, — the starry heavens above and the moral law within." This paramount elevation of the Moral law is what the Psalmist, according to one of the chief peculiarities of the Divine Inspiration of the Bible, urges through the remainder of the Psalm. He tells us how the Law of God (the revealed law of goodness, the natural law of conscience,) is not only what we are bound to follow as our duty, but is the surest source both of our wisdom and our happiness. Not only does he speak of the law as " perfect, converting the soul," " pure," " clean," "true and righteous," — such, perhaps, we all acknowledge it to be, — but it is more than this, " it giveth wisdom unto the simple, it enlightens the eyes." Most true. Many and many a time in life do we see a good and honest conscience supplying a man, young or old, with that common sense, with that discernment, with that calm and impartial judgment, which is often not to be got even from the greatest abilities, or learning, or genius. " The fear of the Lord," — much more the love of God, — " is the beginning " of many other good things; but it certainly is " the beginning of wisdom." Give us a character on which we can thoroughly depend, which we are sure will not fail us in time of need, which we know to be based on principle and on the fear of God, and it is wonderful how many brilliant and popular and splendid qualities we can safely and gladly dispense with. And not only so, but the Psalmist tells us further that the law of God, the submission to the law of God, is the source of our happiness and cheerfulness. He does not only mean that commonplace saying, that virtue is happiness; but he means that the very consciousness of a Divine Law over us to which we submit ourselves is the chief cause of cheerfulness and contentment and peace. The statutes of the Lord "*rejoice* the heart;" they are "*sweeter than honey and the honeycomb.*" There are many perplexities, there are many cares, there are many little vexations in life; what is it which in the midst of these gives us a serene constant cheerfulness and gayety of heart? It is simply remembering that we have a fixed law of duty, a fixed law of our condition in life, which we must fulfil; unchangeable laws which will not endure to be broken, which are our support in time of adversity, no less surely than they are our restraint in time of prosperity. "*Moreover by them,*" he proceeds, as if speaking from the fulness of his own experience, "*is thy servant taught, and in keeping of them there is great reward. Who can tell how oft he offendeth? O cleanse thou me from my secret faults.*" Yes, indeed, this is the prayer for us all; this is the very use of prayer; that He who knows us better than we know ourselves will strengthen us against the sins of which we ourselves are ignorant. "*Keep thy servant also from presumptuous sins; let them not have dominion over me;*" from those headstrong wilful faults that, if indulged, do indeed have dominion over us, such as we cannot shake off. "*So shall I be undefiled and innocent from the great offence.*" This is our reward in keeping from wanton presumptuous carelessness even in trifles; that we are less and less likely to fall into those great offences which destroy soul and body, individuals and nations, with a destruction which, even in this life, makes us shudder and tremble at the thought or the fear of it. And so he concludes, "*Let the words of my mouth and the meditation of my heart be alway acceptable in thy sight,*

O Lord, my strength and my Redeemer." Oh, grant that it may be so with us. I have reminded you, — I would also remind myself, — that this is almost the last Sunday on which I shall have thus to address you in this country and in this manner of life. There are many other things that I would fain say now, many other things that I ought to have said before; but I have thought it best to confine myself to the reflections which this noble Psalm, read beneath the walls of this noble Temple, has suggested. " O, may the words of our mouths," " O, may the meditation of our hearts," on all that we have seen and heard and enjoyed and admired, during these five eventful weeks, be not now only, but always " acceptable in Thy sight, O Lord, our Strength," — the strength of our strength, the help of our weakness, — " O Lord, our Redeemer," — our Redeemer from all danger, from all sin, from all evil, now and hereafter.

SERMON X.
THE LAST ENCAMPMENT.

SERMON X.

THE LAST ENCAMPMENT.

PREACHED IN THE ENCAMPMENT AT EHDEN, BENEATH THE MOUN-
TAIN OF THE CEDARS, ON MAY 11, THE THIRD SUNDAY AFTER
EASTER.

And it came to pass, when the ark set forward, that Moses said, Rise up, Lord, and let thine enemies be scattered; and let them that hate Thee flee before Thee. And when it rested, he said, Return, O Lord, unto the many thousands of Israel.—NUM. x. 35, 36.

OUR last Sunday in Syria has arrived, and it has been enhanced to us this morning by the sight of those venerable trees which seemed to the Psalmist and the Prophets of old one of the chief glories and wonders of the creation. Two main ideas were conveyed to the minds of those who then saw them, which we may still bear away with us.

One is that of their greatness, breadth, solidity, vastness. "The righteous," says the Psalmist,[1] "shall flourish like a palm-tree." That is one part of our life; to be upright, graceful, gentle, like that most beautiful of oriental trees. But there is another quality added, "He shall spread abroad like a cedar in Libanus." That is, his character shall be sturdy, solid, broad; he shall protect others, as well as himself; he shall support the branches of the weaker

[1] Psalm xcii. 12.

trees around him; he shall cover a vast surface of the earth with his shadow; he shall grow and spread and endure; he and his works shall make the place where he was planted memorable for future times.

The second feeling is the value of Reverence. It was reverence for these great trees which caused them to be employed for the sacred service of Solomon's Temple, and which has insured their preservation for so long. It was reverence for Almighty God that caused these trees, and these only, to be brought down from this remote situation to be employed for the Temple of old. Reverence, we may be sure, whether to God or to the great things which God has made in the world, is one of the qualities most needful for every human being, if he means to pass through life in a manner worthy of the place which God has given him in the world.

But the sight of the Cedars, and our encampment here recall to us that this is the close of a manner of life which in many respects calls to mind that of the ancient Israelites, as we read it in the Lessons of this and of last Sunday, in the Book of Numbers and of Deuteronomy, " How goodly are thy tents, O Jacob, and thy tabernacles, O Israel" so unlike our common life, so suggestive of thoughts which can hardly come to us again. It brings us back, even with all the luxuries which surround us, to something of the freshness and rudeness and simplicity of primitive life, which it is good for us all to feel at one time or other. It reminds us, though in a figure, of the uncertainty and instability of human existence, so often compared to the pitching and striking of a tent. The spots on which, day after day for the last six weeks, we have been encamped have again become a desolate open waste, — " the spirit of the desert stalks in," and their place will be known no more. How like the way in which happy homes rise and sink and vanish, and are lost. Only the great Rock or Tree of Life under which they have been pitched remains on from generation to generation.

But there is one point in the encampment of the Israelites which is connected not only with our present mode of life, but with our whole life, wherever we may be, and that is, the words in which were expressed what may be called their Morning and Evening Hymn, their Morning and Evening Prayer. The Morning Prayer was, "*Let God arise, and let His enemies be scattered, and let them that hate Him flee before Him.*" It is very short, but it contains much; and it was used to give fresh point to Jewish Psalms in later times, as, for example, the 68th. It is the call upon God to "rise," as it were, with them, to go forth with them through the day, that "all His enemies might be scattered, and flee before Him," as the shades of night are scattered and flee before the rays of the rising sun. And the Evening Prayer is like to it, only shorter still, — "*Return, O Lord, unto the many thousands of Israel.*" And this, too, is expanded in the 80th Psalm: "Return," come back, our Great Protector, to each several tent as it is pitched again; through all "the many thousands of Israel," not to Judah only, not to Ephraim only; but "before Ephraim, Benjamin, and Manasseh," before Judah and Simeon, before Zebulon and Naphtali, " stir up Thy strength," and be with them all through this night and forever.

So they prayed at each successive start. So we also may well pray at each successive stage of our journey, at the end of one stage and the beginning of another. But there is a yet more general lesson to be learned from these words, over and above any connection with our present journey, applying in the strongest degree to the whole journey of life; and I have reserved it, for this reason, to the end of this stage of our travelling, because it really extends so far more widely, though we are here more specially reminded of it.

May I take this occasion of speaking of the importance of this one solemn ordinance of religion, never to be forgotten, wherever we are, — MORNING AND EVENING PRAYER? It is the best means of reminding ourselves of the presence of God. To place ourselves in His hands before we go forth on our journey, on our pleasure, on our work, — to commit ourselves again to Him before we retire to rest; this is the best security for keeping up our faith and trust in Him in whom we all profess to believe, whom we all expect to meet after we leave this world. It is also the best security for our leading a good and a happy life. It has been well said twice over by the most powerful delineator of human character (with one exception) ever produced by our country,[1] that prayer to the Almighty Searcher of Hearts is the best check to mourners against Providence, or to the inroad of worldly passions, because nothing else brings before us so strongly their inconsistency and unreasonableness. We shall find it twice as difficult to fall into sin, if we

[1] Sir Walter Scott, in the *Talisman* (chap. xxii.), and in *Quentin Durward* (chap. xvii.).

have prayed against it that very morning, or if we thank God for having kept it from us that very evening. It is the best means of gaining strength and refreshment, and courage and self-denial for the day. It is the best means of gaining content and tranquillity and rest for the night; for it brings us, as nothing else can bring us, into the presence of Him who is the source of all these things, and who gives them freely to those who truly and sincerely ask for them. We may "ask" for them without caring to have them; but that is not really "asking." We may "seek," but without lifting up our little finger to get what we seek; but that is not really "seeking." We may "knock," but so feebly and irresolutely that no sound can be heard within or without; that is not really to "knock." But "ask" distinctly and with understanding; "seek" earnestly and deliberately; "knock" eagerly and pertinaciously; and in some way or other, depend upon it, we shall be answered.

I do not wish to lay undue stress on any one of the springs of our moral strength. Like the sacred river of the Holy Land which we have just left, so also the river of our spiritual life has many sources, many springs, unrecognized by man, but recognized by God. All manner of good deeds, good examples, religious forms and institutions, — all these, in their different ways, go to swell the current of our good thoughts. But still to us, as Christians, — to us, I would still more directly say, as Protestant Englishmen, — there are two sources, two springs more especially sacred and important; and these are the fountains of Morning and of Evening Prayer. We have cast off many religious forms to which other nations and other

Churches look for spiritual help; and this makes it the more incumbent upon us to make the most of those which remain to us. We acknowledge the duty, we have learned it from our earliest years; the very practice carries us back to the best days of our childhood. Once lose the habit, and it may be hard to begin again; but once get a firm hold of it, and you will feel that to have left it off for a single morning or a single evening, is like dropping one of your daily employments, like striking off one of your supplies of daily strength, like throwing away one of your best opportunities of being what we ought to be and what we wish to be.

No one can pretend to prescribe what another's prayers should be; that each man must know best for himself. But the general spirit in which they should be offered is well expressed in those two great Prayers of the Israelite encampment of which I have spoken. Whatever may be our particular petitions to God in the morning, we must have this object steadily before us; that He will rise and go forth with us to our daily duties and enjoyments; that He may be in our thoughts throughout the day; and that His enemies may flee before Him, on every occasion when they lurk for us. God's enemies are our enemies; and His enemies and ours are those sins which devour our best dispositions, and destroy our best affections, and corrupt our best hopes and thoughts.

And whatever be our particular petition in the evening, then also we must have no less before us the desire that God will "*return*" to us,—that He will "return" to us, however much we may have offended Him during the day,—that He will forgive us our many shortcomings,—that He will "turn again, and make the light of His countenance to shine upon us" in darkness, in danger, in sorrow, in care,—that He will "return," not only to us, but "to the many thousands of Israel,"—that His blessing may come, not only on us, but on all those, far or near, who go to rest this night in our distant homes, as well as in the several tents of our near encampment.

And I cannot forbear to recall parts at least of the Morning and the Evening Hymns which have been left to us by two men, one long ago passed away, the other still living; both long to be remembered as among the chief ornaments of the English Church; both of whose hymns[1] are worthy to be recalled to our thoughts, even on the frontier of the Holy Land,— even under the shadow of the Cedars of Lebanon.

Morning Hymn.

AWAKE, my soul, and with the sun
Thy daily course of duty run;
Shake off dull sloth, and early rise,
To pay thy morning sacrifice.

Redeem thy misspent moments past,
And live this day as if thy last;
Thy talent to improve take care;
For the great day thyself prepare.

[1] I have here joined together the most universally applicable parts of the Morning and Evening Hymns of Bishop Ken, and of Keble's *Christian Year*.

Let all thy converse be sincere,
Thy conscience as the noon-day clear;
For God's all-seeing eye surveys
Thy secret thoughts, thy works and ways.

Direct, control, suggest, this day,
All I design, or do, or say;
Guard my first springs of thought and will,
And with Thyself my spirit fill.

NEW mercies, each returning day,
Hover around us while we pray;
New perils past, new sins forgiven,
New thoughts of God, new hopes of heaven.

If in our daily course our mind
Be set to hallow all we find,
New treasures still of countless price
God will provide for sacrifice.

The trivial round, the common task,
Will furnish all we ought to ask;
Room to deny ourselves, — a road
To bring us daily nearer God.

Only, O Lord, in Thy dear love
Fit us for perfect rest above;
And help us, this and every day,
To live more nearly as we pray.

Evening Hymn.

GLORY to Thee, my God, this night,
For all the blessings of the light;
Keep me, Oh, keep me, King of kings,
Under Thine own Almighty wings!

Forgive me, Lord, for Thy dear Son,
The ill that I this day have done;
That, with the world, myself, and Thee,
I, ere I sleep, at peace may be.

Teach me to live, that I may dread
The grave as little as my bed;
Teach me to die, that so I may
With joy behold the judgment-day.

Oh, may my soul on Thee repose;
Thou with sweet sleep mine eyelids close;
Sleep that may me more vigorous make
To serve my God when I awake.

ABIDE with me from morn to eve,
For without Thee I cannot live.
Abide with me when night is nigh,
For without Thee I dare not die.

The Rulers of our native land,
'Twixt Thee and us ordained to stand;
Guide Thou their course, O Lord, aright,
Let all do all as in Thy sight.

If some poor wandering child of Thine
Have spurn'd to-day the Voice Divine;
Now, Lord, the gracious work begin,
Let him no more lie down in sin.

Come near and bless us when we wake,
Ere through the world our way we take;
Till, in the ocean of Thy love,
We lose ourselves in Heaven above.

SERMONS IN THE MEDITERRANEAN.

SERMON XI.

S. JOHN AT PATMOS AND AT EPHESUS.

SERMON XI.

S. JOHN AT PATMOS AND AT EPHESUS.

PREACHED ON BOARD H. M. S. "OSBORNE," ON MAY 18, THE FOURTH
SUNDAY AFTER EASTER, ON THE DAY AFTER VISITING PATMOS
AND EPHESUS.

When He, the Spirit of Truth, is come, He will guide you into all truth.
JOHN xvi. 13.

THESE words of our Saviour, recorded by His beloved disciple S. John, in the Gospel of this day, tell us that, when He should be withdrawn, His Spirit would still guide His Apostles to teach to the world the truth which the world most needed to know. We, in the course of yesterday, have been on the track of the very Apostle who wrote down these words for his own support and ours. We have seen at Patmos and at Ephesus the last traces of S. John, with whom we parted, as it were, on the shores of his own lake of Tiberias. Let us ask ourselves what are the lessons which he has left to us? What are the truths, which, without him, we should not have known as clearly as we do now? It is well from time to time to ask this question about each part of the Bible. Let us now ask it with respect to the writings of S. John. There are three portions of the New Testament which have come down to us with the authority of his great name; the

Revelation, written at Patmos, the Gospel and the three Epistles, probably written at Ephesus. Each of these has its own peculiar lesson. Let us take them in order.

I. The Book of the Revelation. Most of this book is very difficult, and for many of us, unnecessary to read. But there are parts which are most edifying: Chapters i. ii. iii. (the Epistles to the Seven Churches amidst which we are now moving); Chapters iv. v. vii xiv. xix. xx. xxi. and xxii. (the judgment of the world, the blessedness of the good, the misery of the wicked). And there is through the whole of the book this great truth, that this life and the next life run into each other; that what we are in the life to come depends on what we are in this life. S. John, in the Revelation, saw the Eternal World revealed in the events of this world. In the trials of the Christian Churches in these islands, and on these shores, he saw the mercy and severity of God leading them on to better things, if only they would obey the call. In the happiness of those who triumphed over temptation and persecution here, he saw the happiness which awaits all good men beyond the grave. In the judgments which befell or which were likely to befall the wicked Roman Empire under which he was living, he saw the likeness of those judgments which will sooner or later fall upon oppression, injustice, impurity, everywhere. This is the first portion of God's truth which we learn from S. John. Always in this life bear about the remembrance of the next. Every event, public or private, that befalls us may be turned, by our own care or our own neglect, to our salvation or our ruin. For every blessing, for every sorrow, for every re-

SERM. XI.] *JOHN AT PATMOS AND EPHESUS.* 111

sponsibility which we have had, God will at last call us to account. The more we can be raised above the petty vexations and pleasures of this world into the Eternal Life to come, the more shall we be prepared to enter into that Eternal Life whenever God shall please to call us hence.

II. The Gospel of S. John. In many respects this Gospel is the same as the other three. But, in one respect especially, it impresses upon us a truth which in the other Gospels we do not see so clearly. It tells us not only how Christ was the Example of man, the likeness of what we ought to be; but it also tells us how He was the Likeness of God, the expression to us of what the Mind of God is in its fullest perfection. "In the beginning was the Word, and the Word was with God, and the Word was God."[1] No man hath seen God at any time; but the only begotten Son, which is in the bosom of the Father, He hath declared Him." "The Word was made flesh and dwelt among us (and we beheld His glory, the glory of the only begotten of the Father), full of grace and truth."[2] This is what is called the doctrine of the Incarnation and of our Lord's Divinity. But it is no mere doctrine of theology. It concerns us all. We all wish to learn what God is like, — we all find it difficult to figure to our minds any idea of the invisible, eternal, omnipresent Father. The old heathens tried to make out His likeness in beautiful statues, or to see it in the works of nature. In the Old Testament we get a truer idea of Him, — that there is but One God, perfectly just and pure. But it is only in the New Testament that we have the fullest revelation of what He

[1] John i. 1.   [2] John i. 14.

is. Read in the Gospels, — read especially in St. John's Gospel, — what Christ was; fix His character in your minds; see how He dealt with sin and with sinners; how he dealt with the religious world, with the irreligious world; observe His loving-kindness, His wisdom, His firmness, His gentleness: this is the nearest approach that has ever been made to bring down the mind of God within the comprehension and the devotion and the worship of men. If you wish to learn how God regards your happiness and cheerfulness, read St. John's account of the marriage feast at Cana. If you wish to learn how He looks upon your sorrows, your trials, your bereavements, look at the 14th, 15th, and 16th chapters of S. John's Gospel, and see how Christ spoke to His sorrowing disciples. If you wish to learn how He regards your sins, look at the union of compassion and disgust with which He speaks to the sinners who come before Him, and with which we ourselves regard those who brought Him to His end.

This is the main object of S. John's Gospel. It fixes our ideas about God. It tells us that goodness and justice and truth, such as we see in Jesus Christ, are the conceptions we ought to have of God. If we are like Christ, we are like God. If Christ is pleased with us, then God is pleased with us. If we know that Christ could not be pleased with us, then we know that God is not pleased with us.

III. The Epistles of S. John. — They are three in number, and they contain many precepts and many doctrines. But there is one doctrine and one precept which they contain more than any other, and which, according to tradition, he repeated over and over again in the market-place of Ephesus, when he was so old that he could say nothing else, and that is, " Little children, love one another." " This," he said to those who complained of hearing nothing else, — " this is the substance of the Gospel. If you " do this, I have nothing further to teach you." *Love one another.* What he meant was, that this is the paramount and crowning duty of the Christian believer. He did not say, as many Christians have said since, " Agree with one another in doctrine." He did not say as many Christians have said, " Hate one another and kill one another." He did not say, " Flatter one another, indulge one another." He did not even say, " Teach one another, inform one another." What he did urge was, that difficult, but necessary, grace, " Love one another." That is, Love one another in spite of your differences, in spite of your faults; do what you can to serve each other, to lighten each other's trials and inconveniences and burdens: above all, if we may turn the precept into its most practical form, Make the best of one another.

" Make the best of one another," he said to the Churches of his own time, and he would say to the Churches of our time, and to those who, like us, are travelling through many Churches and many nations, — " Make the most of what there is good." It is very easy to do the reverse, and to make the most of what there is evil, absurd, erroneous. By so doing we shall have no difficulty in rendering bitterness more bitter, and estrangements between nations and nations and Christians and Christians more wide, and hatreds and strifes more abundant, and errors more extreme. But we shall not be fulfilling the command of Christ, nor of His beloved disciple. No doubt, justice and truth require that we should express our abhorrence of folly and error and sin. But still, by making the most of what there is good, that which is bad will be most likely to disappear. Nothing drives out darkness so much as light; nothing overcomes evil so much as good. No weapon of controversy or argument or opposition is so effectual as when our adversary sees that we see and admire what there is in him that is good and just and right and true.

"Make the best of one another." So also he said to the old and middle-aged and young who crowded round him as he was sinking into his grave under the experience of a hundred eventful years; and so also he still says to us as individuals, in all the relations of life. Here again we may, if we choose, make the worst of one another. Every one has his weak point; every one has his faults; we may make the worst of these; we may fix our attention constantly upon these. It is a very easy task; and by so doing we shall make the burden of life unendurable, and turn friends into enemies, and provoke strife, hatred, heart-burnings, wherever we go, and cut off from ourselves one of the chief sources of happiness and goodness and usefulness. But we may also make the best of one another. We may forgive, even as we hope to be forgiven. We may put ourselves in the place of others, and ask what we should wish to be done to us, and thought of us, were we in their place. By fixing our attention on their good qualities, we shall rise to their level as surely as, by fixing our attention on their bad qualities, we shall sink below their level. By loving whatever is lovable in those around us, love will flow back from them to us, and life will become a pleasure instead of a pain ; and earth will become like Heaven ; and we, if God so please, shall become not unworthy followers of Him whose name is Love, and of St. John his beloved disciple.

SERMON XII.

S. PAUL IN EUROPE.

SERMON XII.

S. PAUL IN EUROPE.

PREACHED ON BOARD H. M. S. "OSBORNE," JUNE 1, OFF THE COAST OF GREECE ON THE WAY FROM ATHENS TO MALTA.

Last of all, he was seen of me also .... that am not meet to be called an Apostle..... But by the grace of God I am what I am .... I labored more abundantly than they all; yet not I, but the grace of God which was with me. — 1 Cor. xv. 8, 9, 10.

WHEN I last addressed you, we had just trodden in the footsteps of the Apostle S. John. We have since entered on the sphere of another Apostle, the last whose history we shall be able to trace in this journey, — the Apostle S. Paul. He — unlike most of the Apostles, who clung to their native East — crossed from Asia to Europe; and for many years of his life, these seas, these islands, these shores were full of his deeds and of his writings. He stood and spoke on the rocky steps of Mars' Hill, at Athens. His Epistles to the Corinthian Church were addressed in fact to the whole of Greece, of which Corinth then, as Athens now, was the capital. He traversed the Mediterranean to and fro; four times on these waters he suffered shipwreck, — a night and a day on these waves he was in the deep. On our own island of Malta he escaped with his life. Through the preaching of his disciples, the Gospel first reached to our shores. He was the Apostle of the Gentiles, but above all, the Apostle of Greece and of Europe. Let us ask, as in the case of S. John, what are the practical lessons we may learn from his life.

I will select four.

I. He was, first, the Apostle, as I have said, of the Gentiles, that is, he urged that into the fold of the Jewish Church should be received those heathen nations who before had been kept out of it. It was the widest extension of the True Religion that had ever been made, or that has ever been made. In order to effect it, he had to struggle against the most obstinate prejudice in his own heart and in the hearts of his countrymen that we can possibly imagine. He was thus the great teacher and the great example of what in one word we call *Toleration*. Toleration of the infirmities, of the errors, of the differences of others, is one of the most difficult of all human virtues. Intolerance is one of the most common and easy of all human vices. But S. Paul has taught us that in order to be religious we need not be intolerant; he has also taught us in what toleration consists. Read his speech to the Athenians, in the 17th chapter of the Acts, read the 14th chapter of the Epistle to the Romans and the 8th of the 1st to the Corinthians, and you will see that the way in which he contrived to attain this great Christian grace was by trying to be as considerate to the scruples and the weaknesses of others as if they were his own; by acknowledging the value of a good motive and a good intention, even when the act itself was mistaken; by recognizing that within the same Christian community wide differences might exist without breaking the bond of Christian fellowship. It is in this respect that the Church of England, to which we belong, is so singularly happy amongst the Churches of the world. It is in this sense the most Protestant and also the most Christian Church in the world, because it is the most comprehensive, and because in this respect it walks and bids us walk in the footsteps of our Lord's great Apostle, S. Paul.

II. This is one lesson of S. Paul's life, both to Jews and Gentiles. Another is his constant protest against the peculiar sins of the heathen world. Because he was indulgent to their weaknesses, he was not therefore indulgent to their sins.

There were many deeply-rooted evils against which he lifted up his voice. I will mention one, namely, that gross sensual wickedness which was so common in heathen times, and which still in our times tempts thousands to their ruin. I know — we all know — how difficult it is to speak of this; and yet the thought that S. Paul has spoken of it as he has, may encourage me to say, and induce you to hear, a few words on what so deeply concerns us all. Perhaps of all the forms of excuse and temptation which this sin assumes, the most common, the most persuasive, is this: that we are but doing as others do; and that what others do we may do. I will not now ask how far the fact is so. I know not — none of us know — how much better or how much worse than they seem our fellow-men may be. But let every one sincerely ask himself whether the conduct of others really makes better what he knows in itself to be wrong and wicked and hateful? Though thousands on thousands fall away,

S. Paul's words of strong condemnation, the truth of which we acknowledge in our own consciences, remains the same.

A bad temper is not more excusable, or less offensive, because others have bad tempers as well as we. A cruel unfeeling act is not less cruel or unfeeling, because others, under strong temptation, have been cruel and unfeeling. The old heathen maxim, "Let us eat and drink, for to-morrow we die," was not less base and contemptible because thousands acted upon it. Neither is the impure word or the unclean act less impure, or less selfish, or less loathsome, or less widely mischievous, because it is shared by numbers around us.

And on the other hand, we know not the wide effects for good, stretching far beyond ourselves, from the firm and silent resistance to this great and sore temptation even by any one single person. We cannot measure the strength and peace and hope and joy which is brought to many and many a troubled soul by the thought of any pure and blameless youth, even in the humblest station of life, struggling manfully and successfully against the evil influences which would lead him astray from the path of innocence. Such characters are indeed the salt of the world, which alone save it from sinking into utter recklessness and universal corruption. May God bless them, whoever and wherever they be, for the inestimable blessing which they unconsciously, but most surely, confer on the world in which their lot is cast.

III. A third lesson of S. Paul's life and doctrine is his deep humility. "By the grace of God I am what I am." "I am the least of the Apostles, that am not worthy to be called an Apostle." It was not that he did not know how great were his gifts; but still he had behind and within a deep-seated feeling of his own shortcomings in times past and present,· of his own profound unworthiness before God, of his constant dependence on the help of others, and, above all, on the help of God. This was a feeling which the Gentile world little appreciated, but it is a feeling which lies at the bottom of all true Christian excellence. To be humble; to be willing to hear of our faults, and to have them corrected; to know that we have that within us which needs to be constantly forgiven; to feel that we are always needing the help of One greater than ourselves, to lead us right; not merely to say that we are miserable sinners, like all the rest of the world, but to acknowledge some special miserable sin of which we have been guilty on one special year and day, and in which we feel that we are guilty as others are not guilty; to be on the watch for every opportunity of improvement and growth in goodness and wisdom, — this is indeed the first beginning of a holy and a happy life, the first requisite to be truly followers of S. Paul.

IV. Fourthly and lastly, there is the Apostle's untiring, unconquerable energy. This is what makes him so exactly suited to be the Apostle of Europe, — which makes us feel that when he passed out of the indolence and inactivity of Asia into this Western world of action and industry and progress, he was for the first time, as it were, in his own element. He "labored more *abundantly*" than they all. Backwards and forwards across these seas, — through danger, through hardship, through heat and cold, through misunderstanding and persecution, in tumults and labors, in solitude and desertion, in spite of sickness and constant weakness, he never flagged; he left no stone unturned to do the work which was set before him. And what was that work? In the scenes and the recollections of these countries which for some of us have so vast an interest, he had little or none. Great as those recollections are, his own recollections were greater still. His work was to labor in his Master's cause. It was to do good to his fellow-creatures; it was to render them better and wiser, to bring them more near to God, and make them more like to Christ. My brethren, although we are not Apostles, yet His work is really ours, and His energy ought in some measure to be ours also. To us, as to Him, these visits to the famous and beautiful places of the earth are, after all, but the play and the ornament of life. Whether we now care for these things much or little, they are not on earth our main business. Our main business is in our own professions, our own homes, — our European life, our English life, — our own special vocation, whatever it be, whether on sea or on land; above all, in that vocation which is common to all of us, — the vocation of Christians, of being good ourselves and doing good to others. These are interests which demand our utmost energy always. These are interests which never fail. This is an energy which is required the more imperatively as we approach our homes, as we return to our settled mode of life, as we look backward to all that we there have left undone hitherto, as we look forward to all that there remains to be done in the time to come. *We are not indolent Asiatics, but active Englishmen;* we are not Mussulmans, who place their chief duty in passive resignation, but Christians, who know that the chief duty of men is the active service of God and mankind; we have for our example, not the repose of heathen philosophers, but the untiring devotion and exertion of the Christian Apostle. In his name, and in his Master's name, let us gird ourselves up to be worthy of our high calling,—"*always abounding*[1] *in the work*," whatever it be, the constant, unfailing work which God has given us to do, "*knowing that our labor*," however toilsome, however irksome, however thankless, on earth, shall not be "*in vain*," and is not "in vain" in the sight of Christ our Lord.

[1] 1 Cor. xv. 58.

SERMON XIII.
THE GIFT OF THE SPIRIT.

(WHITSUNDAY.)

SERMON XIII.

THE GIFT OF THE SPIRIT.

PREACHED ON BOARD H. M. S. "OSBORNE," ON WHITSUNDAY, JUNE 8, BETWEEN MALTA AND MARSEILLES.

The Comforter, which is the Holy Spirit, whom the Father will send in My name, he shall teach you all things. Peace I leave with you, My peace I give unto you: not as the world giveth, give I unto you.
JOHN xiv. 26, 27.

THIS is the great Festival of Whitsunday. It is the Festival of the Holy Spirit. It tells us of the last and parting gift of our Lord to His apostles, to all generations of mankind forever. What is this gift? What do we learn from the way in which it is spoken of in the Bible and in the services of this day? I will confine myself to what the word itself suggests. This is a very useful and easy mode of studying the depths of the wisdom of the Bible. The words, the names which it uses to describe the great truths which it has to teach, are so full of meaning, that we need but draw out that meaning, and we shall find what we want.

1. The *Spirit* of Christ. — This is what we have to ask and to imitate; not the letter, not the mere outward likeness, but the *spirit*, the intention of His actions, is what He wishes to give us, and what we must earnestly seek for. Though He was poor,

whereas we may be rich; though He went about teaching, whereas we perhaps never teach at all; though He lived and died in one small country ages ago, whilst we have traversed many countries, and live in times wholly different, yet we still may be like Him; we still may be in communion with Him, because what we aim at is the mind, the soul, the Spirit which breathed through all His life, and which can be shared in a measure by every one of us. This is the best use of this sense of the word; but it is useful as a guide of life generally. To this end must we always distinguish between the spirit and the letter, and see how the spirit is always more important than the letter. Many difficulties in the Bible, which perplex us when we look only at the mere letter, vanish away when we look at the general spirit. Many stumbling-blocks which meet us in particular portions of the services of the Church, or in the institutions of our country, are at once surmounted when we think of the spirit of the whole. Many dispensations of Providence, which seem grievous to be borne, become light when, from the mere letter and fact which kill, we can feel through them the gracious Spirit that gives life and strength and healing to what in itself is dark and mournful. And in our own hearts, when we pray for the Spirit of Christ to enlighten us, what we pray for is that He will enlighten and purify not only our outward acts, but the innermost springs of our inmost mind and conscience and spirit. Through our spirits only can God now speak to us as a Spirit. It is to our spiritual life that we must pay heed, if we wish not to be cut off from Him.

2. Again, the *Spirit* of Christ is that which enlivens,

strengthens, invigorates. — We speak, and we speak properly, of a "man of spirit," of a "boy of spirit," of a "high, bold, gallant spirit." This is another sense of the word "Spirit" in the Bible. It signifies "breath" or "wind." "The wind bloweth where it listeth, and thou hearest the sound thereof," . . . "so is every one that is born of the Spirit." As is the fresh breeze to a ship becalmed at sea, filling her sails, and driving her onwards in spite of herself, so is the Spirit of God and of Christ to the torpid, languid human soul, which will not be roused except by a power greater and higher than itself. As is the fresh air to a close infected room, so is the keen, invigorating breeze from the throne of God, which pours into the narrow chamber of the heart, stuffed with the prejudices and passions and fancies of our own little circle, of our own little thoughts, whose doors have never been opened to new ideas or bright feelings, whose windows have been closed against all wider and higher views.

Such was the "Spirit of the Lord" which "came" on the heroes and saints of the old dispensation, — Gideon, Samson, and David, — and filled them with strength for the battle. Such was the "rushing mighty wind," in the Christian Church, which, from the day of Pentecost onwards, swept through the dead dry bones of the ancient world, and roused them to life. Such was the spirit of those old Christian knights, the scene of whose deeds we have lately visited, who made it the business of their lives to defend with a soldier's courage and fidelity the weak, the suffering, and the oppressed everywhere. Such, above all, was the soldier-like spirit of Him who was the Captain of our salvation, who fought to the last with unabated, unshrinking courage His battle, our battle, the battle of the whole world, against sin and folly and death. Oh for one spark of this soldier-like spirit in the weak and wavering moments of our daily course! Oh for one breath of this divine atmosphere of the Spirit to brace our nerves, and enliven our sluggish, sinking hearts, and chase away the sultry oppression that weighs us down in the great struggles of life! Oh for one blast of that rushing mighty wind, to drive us with irresistible force over wave after wave of this troublesome world, till we come to the haven where we would be! The Spirit of God and of Christ is life and strength and health and energy; where these are not, there only in a very feeble degree is the breath of God's Spirit.

3. The "Spirit of God" in the Bible is often used in another sense, which perhaps we do not enough connect with it, — that sense in which it is used in the Confirmation Service, and in the 11th chapter just read from the Prophet Isaiah, — "*the Spirit of wisdom and understanding and knowledge;*" and so in the Collect of this day, we pray that "we may, through the Spirit, have a *right judgment* in all things;" and so our Lord speaks of "the Spirit of *Truth*, which shall lead His followers into all *truth*." This is a most important characteristic of the Divine Spirit, which we ought to ask from God, because often wisdom and religion have been parted from each other, and religious zeal and common sense have regarded each other with suspicion. But, in fact, they are most nearly allied. Common sense, discretion, judgment, are high Christian graces. They are God's gifts, to enable us to do the work which is set before us. To be able to

see the truth, and to discern the false from the true, and to wish to know the truth, this is a gift which is needed by the highest philosopher; but it is needed also by the humblest man or youth that has to make his way in life, and to serve his God and his country faithfully and truly. And of all wisdom, of all judgment, the best source is the fear of the Lord. Wickedness is in itself folly,—sheer, miserable folly. Goodness is in itself wisdom, because it gives us a straightforward, independent, fearless judgment, when many abler or more learned men, as the world thinks them, are led astray by interest, or selfishness, or jealousy, or suspicion. Christ, who is " our righteousness and Sanctification and Redemption," is also, as the Apostle tells us, and as we see from His own words, which he spake as never man spake, " our Wisdom." Let us seek His own Spirit from Him, and that which He had without measure He will, in some measure, if we persevere, freely give to the humblest of His followers.

4. Finally, let us remember that this great gift of the Spirit of God was Christ's last gift and consolation to His disciples when he parted from them. He said (using the common word for salutation or farewell in his time and country), "*Peace* I leave with you;" but He added, "*My Peace* I give unto you; *not as the world giveth, give I unto you.*" The peace which He gave was not the superficial congratulation and courtesy of worldly life, but the deep, solid peace which can only come from the Holy, the Pure, and the Strong, dwelling in our spirits, and giving to us His own Holiness and Purity and Strength.

Oh, my brethren, as we part to-day, many of us not to meet again as heretofore for another Sunday's worship, may this be our parting farewell and wish one for another, — may we know what it is to have for our Comforter, in our hearts, and in the hearts of our friends not the peace, the friendship, the spirit of the world, but the peace, the friendship, the Spirit which Christ alone can give. There is the hollow peace, the treacherous friendship, the shifting favor, which the world gives, and which the world, as it knows full well, can take away. But there is, on the other hand, the firm peace of our own consciences, which we cannot lose but through our own fault. There is the faithful and steadfast friendship, which can only be broken off by our own folly. There is the all-sufficient, all-protecting grace of Christ, who will continue to help us so long as we help ourselves, and will never leave us nor forsake us, unless we deliberately leave and forsake Him. O may we all of us, as time rolls on, have "the right judgment" to see and to choose the better part, which neither life, nor death, nor things present, nor things to come, can take from us. As difficulties unforeseen close round us, — as temptations multiply, — as wrong constructions are put on our actions, — as friends fall away, or familiar places become vacant, — as losses and bereavements come thick upon us, — may we have the grace to know and to feel the immeasurable difference between the false and miserable spirit of this hard and selfish world, and the loving, discriminating, generous, holy Spirit, of Christ our merciful Saviour, and of His faithful servants!

SERMON XIV.

THE BREADTH OF GOD'S COMMANDMENT.

[This Sermon, preached on the day following the return of His Royal Highness to England, I have ventured to print in this place, as forming the natural conclusion of the Series.]

SERMON XIV.

THE BREADTH OF GOD'S COMMANDMENT.

PREACHED IN THE PRIVATE CHAPEL OF WINDSOR CASTLE, ON
TRINITY SUNDAY, JUNE 15.

I see that all things come to an end, but thy commandment is exceeding
broad. — PSALM cxix. 96.

THE Psalmist throughout the whole of this Psalm labors, in every variety of form, to express his conviction of the value, — the authority, — the excellence, of what is called by the various terms of "the law," — "the commandment," — "the statutes," — "the testimonies of God." What was the precise idea intended to be conveyed by these different names it is difficult for us to determine at this distance of time, and in the absence of any direct explanation from the Psalmist himself; but, from the general tenor of the Psalm, we cannot be mistaken in supposing that they cover, at any rate, two leading thoughts : — first, and chiefly, the moral Law of duty; and, secondly, and as connected with and based upon this, the Revelation or Dispensation of God. The two are, in fact, in his mind, inseparable, as we shall see, if we follow, verse by verse, the various expressions of rapture, indignation, contrition, awe, reverence, and love which the various phases of the Law excite in his mind.

Amongst all the characteristics which he thus gives, one of the most striking is that in the text. "*I see that all things come to an end,*" — I see that everything else has an abrupt termination, a limitation, a point beyond which you cannot push or apply it; a narrowness, a littleness, an insufficiency, — "*but Thy commandment is exceeding broad.*" It reaches as far as we can see backwards and forwards; it includes all besides, it outlives all besides, it comprehends all besides.

There is an ancient tradition, that Abraham, as he stood on the hills above Damascus, was converted to the true faith in one God, from the worship of the heavenly bodies, by observing that the stars, the moon, and the sun, however bright and glorious, at last sank, and were succeeded by others. "I like not," he said, "those that set;" and so turned to the one unchangeable Lord and Maker of all. This, but in a higher and more precise form, is the force of the Psalmist's argument. He prefers, — and we ought to prefer, — the Commandment, the Revelation, of God, not only because it lasts longer than anything else, but because it includes and comprehends and absorbs into itself all that there is good in everything else.

It is exactly this aspect of Divine Revelation which is brought before us in the ancient doctrine of the Church which we this day commemorate. The doctrine of the Trinity, when rightly understood, impresses upon us, beyond all other doctrines, the Infinity, the Immensity of the Godhead, of Revelation, of Truth, of God's Word, and of God's Commandment. Its very claim to be considered as the crowning doctrine of Christianity rests upon this, — that it includes and embraces all other doctrines and opinions about the nature of God that have ever existed in the Church. The theological part of this great argument I leave untouched; but it may be well to see, practically, in how many instances we are sustained and guided and comforted by this reflection of the breadth, the immensity, the vastness of God's Commandment and of God's Revelation.

1. "I see that all things come to an end." So we may say of all human institutions and customs, especially when we have gone through many lands, and seen many forms of opinion and worship. "I see that there is a boundary beyond which they cannot pass,"— I see that the institutions of the West come to an end almost abruptly when they reach the extremity of Europe. I see that the institutions of the East come to an end no less abruptly when they reach the extremity of Asia. We have followed each to their utmost limit; they cannot pass farther. But there is one thing which is broad enough to embrace them both and cross them both, namely, the Commandment of God. Go where we will, through East or West, the moral Law of God, as written in the hearts of men, is still found the one bond of human brotherhood. Amidst all other differences, justice, purity, generosity, truth, though they meet with different degrees of appreciation, yet do still claim everywhere our respect and reverence and the respect and reverence of others. And yet more than this: go where we will, we shall find that true Christianity — for the very reason that it is based on the moral law, and lays the whole stress of religious teaching upon it — is capable of addressing itself to the most diverse forms of the human race.

It came from Asia: it has taken root in Europe. "Christendom" is not merely a geographical expression. Its boundaries are not confined to the place of its birth nor to the scenes of its subsequent establishment. No single Church can claim for itself the graces of the whole. No single creed has exhausted the whole of Christian truth. We may dwell with pleasure, with comfort, on the goodness and the truth which prevail in each. When we return to our own Church, we may thank God that it is large enough and generous enough to have a place for all who love the Lord Jesus Christ and wish to serve Him faithfully. When we return to our own country, to our own duties, to our own homes, we may thankfully remember that Christ is here as well as there; that, though there, He is also here, — to be loved and followed and adored here, as faithfully as ever in former times He was loved and adored and followed there.

2. This is the most general sense in which these words are true. But they are also true in all the special relations of life. "I see that all things come to an end." "I see that all earthly pleasures and enjoyments, one after another, have their natural ending." Not only wicked and selfish pleasures, which last only for the moment of their gratification, but innocent, just, good enjoyments, of necessity come to an end, or pass into something else. One kind of enjoyment succeeds to another, one occupation treads on another's heels. The journey of life, like the actual journey of travellers, is broken up again and again. One scene puts another out of our recollection. "But the commandment of God is exceeding broad." Through all this complicated web there is one golden

thread, which runs on without breaking, and that is the thread of duty, which is the thread of honor and usefulness and happiness. This leads us into spheres which go on enlarging and enlarging still, with every step in life. Unlike that story of the iron shroud or room, which enclosed its prisoner, day by day, within a narrower and narrower circle, the chamber of duty and of God's commandment widens and opens and expands with new interests, new enjoyments, new affections, new hopes, at every successive step we take, till we find ourselves at last in that Presence, where there is indeed "fulness of joy and pleasure for evermore."

3. Again, "I see that all human greatness comes to an end." Every station in life, however great or however prosperous, has its drawbacks, its checks, its limits. It depends on circumstances over which we have no control, and which may crumble beneath our feet; it depends on popular favor, which may cease; on friends who may fall away, on enemies who are watching for our overthrow; on the chances of advancement; on the life, or the health, or the caprice, of ourselves or of others. But moral or Christian greatness is "exceeding broad." The basis on which it is built up is as broad and firm as the conscience and heart of man, as the grace and goodness of God. It cuts across all other divisions of life. A good deed, a Christian feeling, can cheer us when nothing else can cheer us, — can support us when nothing else can support us, — can give a zest to happiness, which not to have is not to have happiness at all; which in adversity can console us when every other kind of comfort is useless.

4. Again, "I see that all things come to an end." Even the most far-reaching intellect and its effects come to an end at last. Look at those greatest of all monuments of the mind of man, — books. How rapidly they come to an end! How often it happens that the very characteristic which insures to a book its fame for this year or this century, is the very cause of its passing away in the next! One Book alone has outlasted many generations, in all nations equally, and that is the Bible; and this is because of its "exceeding breadth," — because it embraces every variety and element of thought, and every phase of society; above all, because it embodies in every part the moral commandment of God, which endures forever in Heaven, and which speaks not to one condition of life only, but to all.

5. Again, "I see that all human characters come to an end." How often do we see those who are good and wise up to a certain point, but beyond that we come, as it were, to a precipice, — they break down, as we say; we wonder that, being so good as they are, they are not better, that, being as wise as they are, they are not wiser. One Character there is which is so "exceeding broad," as to grasp and overlap all others. This is the true sign of the Divinity of the Character of Christ. It is the personification not of one part only, but of the whole of the Law of God. It has not the littleness of a mere teacher, nor the narrowness of a hermit or a saint, nor the eccentricity of genius. "His shoulder," as the Prophet says, is broad enough "to bear the government" and the sins of the whole world. His mind is wide enough to sympathize with all our infirmities,

as well as with all our efforts after good in every direction. No griefs of life are more trying than those which arise from the half-goodness or the half-wisdom of those whom we wish to love and respect. It is when we think of these things, that the Perfect Law and the Perfect Mind of Christ is so inexpressibly consoling. "Come unto me, all ye that labor and are heavy laden, and *I* will give you rest." Come unto Him, and in His greatness we shall find the enlargement of our littleness, in His tenderness we shall find the softening of our harshness, in His compassion we shall find the lightening of our burden. "I said, It is mine own infirmity; but I will remember the years of the right hand of the Most Highest."

6. Again, "I see that human life comes to an end." Our earthly life, the earthly life of those whom we have known and loved, is cut short by that dark abyss into which we cannot penetrate, and over which our thoughts can hardly pass. But God's commandment, and the fulfilment of God's commandments, is "exceeding broad;" it is broad enough to span even that wide and deep river which parts this life and the next. For it is this which makes this life and the next life one. Knowledge, prophecies, gift of all kinds pass away, but the Love of God and the Love of man never fail. They continue into the unseen world beyond the grave; the remembrance of these things, as we have known them here, enables us still to think of them there; the unselfish purpose, the generous sympathy, the deep affection, the transparent sincerity, the long self-control, the simple humility, of those to whom the Commandment of God has been precious, — these are the arches of that bridge, on which our thoughts and

hopes cross and recross the widest and most mysterious of all the chasms which divide us; the gulf which divides the dead and the living, the gulf which divides God and man.

7. Yes, "I see that all things come to an end." I see that human systems, human pleasures, human greatness, human wisdom, human excellence, human life, come to an end. But the Commandment, the Revelation of God never comes to an end, because God Himself is Infinite, — God, whom we this day adore in His Three Infinite Perfections. So let us conclude with that Apostolic benediction which, in summing up those Divine Perfections, expresses all that any human being can wish for another in the welcomes or the partings of life, — "*the Love of God, the Grace of our Lord Jesus Christ, the Fellowship of the Holy Ghost.*"

The "*Love of God*" our Father never comes to an end. In every dispensation, sorrowful or joyful — in every duty, in every trial — in the great waters, in the heaven of heavens — in our manifold blessings — in our laughter, in our tears, in the fulness of health, in the darkness of the grave — the Hand of God is with us; His love is with us; — and may it be with us always.

"The *Grace of our Lord Jesus Christ*" never comes to an end. The "grace" the beauty, the loveliness of His character is infinite. The "grace" the favor, the good-will, which He alone can give, is far beyond all human popularity, above all human praise, and worth all human judgment. The "grace," the forgiveness, the mercy, which we all so much need, which we are all so unwilling to give to others, — this in our loving Saviour is "exceeding broad," granted to the first beginning of repentance, giving welcome to the humblest of our efforts after good. May this grace of Christ our Lord be with us now and always!

And "*the Fellowship of the Holy Ghost,*" the communion of the Holy Spirit — this also has no end. It has no end, no limit, except that which our own selfishness, or sin, or folly, puts in its way. The fellowship, the communion, in good thoughts, in good deeds, in wise words, — the interchange of loving hearts, and the combination for noble objects, and the coöperation for one another's welfare, and the approval of those whom we love and honor, — this is a fellowship which reaches across all differences of time and place and station and tastes and character; which reaches to the very verge of the grave, and beyond the grave, — for it is the fellowship of the Eternal Spirit of God Himself. May this communion and fellowship be with us and remain with us always, and bind us ever closer and closer to each other and to God!

NOTICES

OF SOME LOCALITIES IN THE EAST

VISITED BY HIS ROYAL HIGHNESS THE PRINCE OF WALES, IN 1862.

INTRODUCTION.
I. THE MOSQUE OF HEBRON.
II. THE SAMARITAN PASSOVER.
III. GALILEE.
IV. HERMON AND LEBANON.
V. PATMOS.

INTRODUCTION.

I HAVE already stated in the Preface to this volume, that the following Notices do not pretend to anything like a continuous narrative of His Royal Highness's journey. They are intended simply to record some of the scenes peculiar to the occasion, and to furnish a few additional illustrations to works already published.

The tour of the Prince of Wales was originally to have included Greece, Egypt, Palestine, and Constantinople. The delay, occasioned by the death of the lamented Prince Consort, necessitated the omission of Greece from the earlier stage of the tour, which thus, after a rapid journey through Europe, and brief visits to the most remarkable spots in the Adriatic, may be said to have begun with Egypt. In Egypt, between Alexandria and the First Cataract, were spent the three first weeks of March. The voyage of the Prince up the Nile was facilitated in every way by the munificent hospitality of the late Viceroy, and he was thus enabled in a very short space of time to see the chief wonders of Egypt, — the Pyramids, Esneh, Philæ, Edfou, Thebes, Dendera, Memphis, Cairo, Suez. To my own former impressions of Egypt I have but little to add. Yet there are two points on which I would touch for a moment. The first is the melancholy thought, that ours is probably the last generation which will be permitted to see the glory of the Egyptian sculptures, as they were first revealed to the explorers of the beginning of this century. Even within the nine years which elapsed between my two visits, the smoke of travellers' torches, and the disfigurement by travellers' names, and the injury by travellers' spoliations, have rendered " the fine gold dim " in many of the paintings and inscriptions; in another fifty years it is probable that many of them will be almost undecipherable. But, on the other hand, the excavation of the ancient monuments had in the same interval brought to light so much, and promises to do so much more, that, as I have elsewhere expressed a hope, the study of Egyptian History has still a large field in prospect. One such result is to be seen in the statues in the museum at Cairo, collected by M. Mariette. Amongst them (to select only one) is the oldest statue, or at least the representation of the oldest known countenance in the world, — *Chephren*, the builder of the Second Pyramid. No one who has seen it can lose the recollection of his singularly expressive features, his strong protruding mouth, his immovable head, supported and protected by the claws and wings of the Sacred Hawk, the Bird of the Sun. Another result, on a larger scale, is the Temple of Edfou. Formerly it was choked up by the mud-huts of an Egyptian village, the heads of the sculptured gods, and the capitals of the vast pillars just emerging from the piles of sand and rubbish. M. Mariette, in 1859, had been sent by the Viceroy to clear it out. The peasants refused to move. He drew a trench round the Temple, and reduced them by blockade.

The villagers surrendered, and the village was transplanted to the outside. Now, as one looks from the top of the gigantic towers, the whole edifice stands out more perfect in all its parts than any deserted abbey of Western Europe. Three points struck me particularly as illustrative of the ancient Egyptian worship. There was the same complexity and multiplication of chambers, staircases, and passages, to and fro, as that exhibited in any mediæval cathedral; even down to the small closets or vestries, with cupboards and recesses for the sacred vestments. There was the innermost sanctuary, standing (as may be seen, though less clearly, at Karnak and Luxor) quite distinct from everything adjoining; a space, as in the Jewish Holy of Holies, drawn round it, evidently to prevent it from coming into contact with any part even of the Temple itself. There was in this sanctuary a huge granite shrine, such as is seen nowhere else in Egypt, but such as must in some form have existed everywhere. It stands by itself, the marks of the door or grate still visible in the entrance, which doubtless enclosed the sacred animal, — probably the Sacred Hawk, — the representative of the Deity of the Temple.

We returned to Cairo on the evening of Sunday, the 23d of March. . . . . In the course of that week the Prince of Wales embarked from Alexandria for Palestine, and at its close, arrived at Jaffa, where we disembarked on the 31st March.

In the journey through the Holy Land, from which the following Notices are chiefly taken, it will readily be understood that, whilst the general characteristics of the tour were those which would have belonged to the passage of any other English traveller, there were some which were peculiar to this journey, and which thus revived again and again the thought that, since the time of Prince Edward and Eleanor, this was the first visit paid by an heir of the Crown of England to these sacred regions.

That long cavalcade, sometimes amounting to a hundred and fifty persons, of the Prince and his suite, the English servants, the troop of fifty or a hundred Turkish cavalry, their spears glittering in the sun, and their red pennons streaming in the air, as they wound their way through the rocks and thickets, and over the stony ridges of Syria, was a sight that enlivened even the tamest landscape, and lent a new charm even to the most beautiful. Most remarkably was this felt on our first entrance into Palestine, and on our first approach to Jerusalem. The entrance of the Prince into the Holy Land was almost on the footsteps of Richard Cœur de Lion, and of Edward I. under the tower of Ramleh and in the ruined cathedral of S. George, at Lydda. Thence we had climbed the pass of Joshua's victory at Beth-horon,[1] had caught the first glimpse of Jerusalem from the top of the Mosque of the Prophet Samuel, where Richard had stood and refused to look on the Holy Sepulchre which he was not thought worthy to rescue. Then came the full view of the Holy City from the northern road, the ridge of Scopus,[2] — the view immortalized in Tasso's description of the first advance of the Crusaders. The cavalcade had now swelled into a strange and motley crowd. The Turkish Governor and his suite, — the English Consul and the English clergy, — groups of uncouth

---

[1] See *Sinai and Palestine*, c. iv. 210, 214.   [2] *Ibid.* c. iii. 186.

Jews, — Franciscan monks and Greek priests, — here and there under the clumps of trees, groups of children singing hymns, — the stragglers at last becoming a mob, — the clatter of the horses' hoofs on the hard stones of that rocky and broken road drowning every other sound, — such was the varied procession, which, barbarous as it was, still seemed to contain within itself the representatives, or, if one will, the offscourings of all nations, and thus to combine the impressive, and, at the same time, the grotesque and melancholy aspect which so peculiarly marks the modern Jerusalem.

Our tents were pitched outside the Damascus Gate, near the scene of the encampment of Godfrey de Bouillon, and from thence we explored the city and the neighborhood.

THE MOSQUE OF HEBRON.

SKETCH PLAN OF THE MOSQUE AT HEBRON.

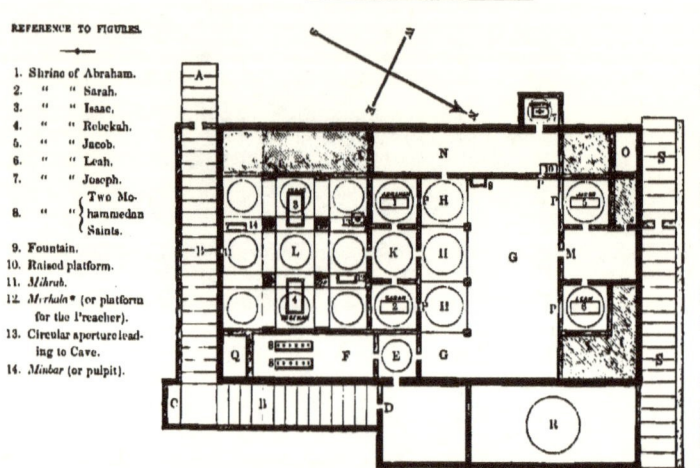

REFERENCE TO FIGURES.

1. Shrine of Abraham.
2. "   " Sarah.
3. "   " Isaac.
4. "   " Rebekah.
5. "   " Jacob.
6. "   " Leah.
7. "   " Joseph.
8. "   " { Two Mohammedan Saints.
9. Fountain.
10. Raised platform.
11. *Mihrab.*
12. *Merhuln** (or platform for the Preacher).
13. Circular aperture leading to Cave.
14. *Minbar* (or pulpit).

REFERENCE TO LETTERS.

A. Flight of Steps to outer door.
B. Long narrow passage of easy steps, bounded on the left by ancient Jewish wall.
C. Fountain.
D. Here Shoes are left at the door of a ceiled room.
E. Passage Chamber.
F. Mosque, containing two Shrines.
G. Outer Court.
H. Cloister of round arches, with domed roof. — The Outer Narthex.
K. Inner Narthex.
L. Nave of Byzantine Church.
M. Long, lofty Room, leading to circular Chambers, containing Shrines of Jacob and Leah.
N. Do., to that containing Shrine of Joseph.
O. Minaret.
P. Windows.
Q. Minaret.
R. The Jáwallyeh Mosque, built by Jáwali.
S. Supplementary Staircase running up the N.W. wall.

N. B. — The deep black lines mark the ancient Jewish Wall. The shaded parts are unknown.

The accompanying Plan was drawn up by my friend and fellow-traveller, the Hon. R. H. Meade, with the assistance of Dr. Rosen, immediately after the visit to the Mosque. It may be compared with the Sketches of the Mosque, given from the information of Mussulmans, in Osburn's *Palestine Past and Present*, and in the *Travels of Ali Bey*. I have also compared it with an unpublished Plan shown to me by the kindness of M. Pierotti. Between these various sketches there are several points of difference. But it has been thought best to give Mr. Meade's Plan as it was drawn up at the time, independently of any other authority.

* This platform in Egyptian Mosques is called *Dikkeh* (see Lane's *Modern Egyptians*, i. 116). The word *Merhula* (or, as it appears in the *Travels of Ali Bey*, *Mehrel*) is, as I am informed by Mr. Laur, not, within his knowledge, applied to this kind of platform. It was, however, certainly used for the platform at Hebron by the Guardians of the Mosque, and, as it properly means a stage, resting-place, or goal of a journey, it may have been used in connection with the final resting-place of the Patriarchs' earthly remains. Mr. Cyril Graham informs me that he has heard the word in this specific sense applied by the Bedawin of the tribe Metlek, east of the Haurân, who hold very holy the *Merhalut* of a certain Lady *Nimreh*, *bint en namir*, who lies buried in a castle on an island in the Wadi *En Nemarch.*

I. THE MOSQUE OF HEBRON.

THERE were formerly four sanctuaries in Palestine, which Mussulman jealousy carefully guarded from the approach of Christians. These were the Mosque of Omar and the Mosque of David at Jerusalem, the Great Mosque at Damascus, and the Mosque of Hebron. Of these, however, the first and third had within the last few years become accessible, and to these every facility of access was given to the Prince of Wales on the present occasion. The second was of too dubious a character (as will be presently noticed) to justify any strong demand for its inspection. But the fourth, the Mosque of Hebron, — in other words the Sanctuary, first Jewish, then Christian, now Mussulman, which is supposed to cover the Cave of Machpelah, — is, of all the Holy Places in Palestine, the one which has excited in modern times the keenest curiosity, and which at the same time rests on the best historical evidence. When on the eve of my first visit to Palestine in 1852, I saw the great German geographer, Ritter, this was the point to which he most earnestly invited my attention. When in the course of that journey we reached Hebron, it was with reluctance that we abandoned, as a total impossibility, the hope of penetrating within that inaccessible sanctuary. It is through the effort made by the Prince of Wales in his journey of 1862, that this wish has, so far as circumstances could admit, been at last gratified, and the success which crowned this effort gave to his Eastern pilgrimage a peculiar value such as has been attached to the visit of no other European Prince to the Holy Land.

It will be well first to indicate the extraordinary interest which attaches to the spot.

The Cave of Machpelah is described in the Book of Genesis with a particularity almost resembling that of a legal deed. The name of "Machpelah," or rather "the Machpelah," appears to have belonged to the whole district or property,[1] though it is applied sometimes to the cave,[2] and sometimes to the field.[3] The meaning of the word is quite uncertain, though that of "double,"[4] which is adopted in all the ancient versions (almost always as if applied to the cave) is the most probable. In this "Machpelah" was a field, "a cultivated field," which belonged not to one of the Amorite chiefs, — Aner, Eshcol, or Mamre, — but to a Hittite, Ephron the son of Zohar.[5] The field was planted, as most of those around the vale of Hebron, with trees; olives, terebinths, or ilexes. At one "end,"[6] probably the upper end, was a cave. The whole place was in the face[7] of "Mamre," that is, as it would seem, opposite

The Cave of Machpelah.

---

[1] Gen. xxiii. 17. "The field of Ephron, which was in Machpelah."
[2] *Ibid.* 9; xxv. 9. "The cave of (the) Machpelah."
[3] Gen. xxiii. 19; xlix. 30; l. 13. "The field of (the) Machpelah."
[4] "Spelunca duplex," Vulgate. τὸ σπήλαιον, τὸ διπλοῦν, LXX. *passim.* Syriac, *passim*, except in Gen. l. 13, where it is rendered "the double field."
[5] Gen. xxiii. 8; xxv. 9.
[6] Gen. xxiii. 9.
[7] This interpretation of the words "before" or "in the face of" Mamre, would require that Mamre should be on the hill immediately to the south

the oaks or terebinths of Mamre, the Amorite, where Abraham had pitched his tent. In this case, it would be immediately within view of his encampment; and the open mouth of the cave may be supposed to have attracted his attention long before he made the proposal which ended in his purchase of this, his first and only property in the Holy Land. "There they buried Abraham and Sarah his wife; there they buried Isaac and Rebekah his wife; and there," according to the dying speech of the last of the Patriarchs, "Jacob buried Leah;" and there he himself was buried[1] "in the cave of the field of Machpelah, which Abraham bought for a possession of a burial-place from Ephron the Hittite before Mamre."[2]

This is the last Biblical notice of the Cave of Machpelah. After the close of the Book of Genesis, no mention is made of it in the Scriptures. Even in the New Testament, in the speech of Stephen,[3] by a singular variation, the tomb at Shechem is substituted for it. It is not even mentioned in the account of Caleb's conquest of Hebron, nor of David's reign there. The only possible allusion is the statement in Absalom's life,[4] that he had vowed a pilgrimage to Hebron.

But the formal and constant reference to it in the Book of Genesis is a sufficient guarantee not only for a spot of that name having existed from early times, but

of the modern town of Hebron. It must be admitted that such a position is inconsistent with the traditional locality either of the existing "oak" of Abraham, or (what is more important) of the place of the sacred "terebinth" worshipped as the spot of his encampment, five miles to the north of Hebron. The Vulgate translates the words, "*e regione*."

[1] Gen. xlix. 30. [3] Acts vii. 16.
[2] *Ibid.* l. 13. [4] 2 Sam. xv. 7.

also for its having been known at the time of the composition of the Book, and of its introduction into the Jewish Canon. That cannot be earlier, on any hypothesis, than the time of Moses, nor later than the times of the Monarchy.

We are not left, however, entirely in the dark. Josephus, in his "Antiquities," tells us that there were [1] "monuments built there by Abraham and his descendants;" and in his "Jewish War," that "the monuments of Abraham and his sons" (apparently alluding to those already mentioned in the Antiquities), "were still shown at Hebron, of beautiful marble, and admirably worked."[2] These monuments[3] can hardly be other than what the "Bourdeaux Pilgrim," in A. D. 333, describes as "a quadrangle of stones of astonishing beauty;" and these again are clearly those which exist at the present day, — the massive enclosure of the Mosque. The tradition, thus carried up unquestionably to the age of Josephus, is in fact carried by the same argument much higher. For the walls, as they now stand, and as Josephus speaks of them, must have been built before his time. The terms which he uses imply this; and he omits to mention them amongst the works of Herod the Great, the only potentate who could or would have built them in his time, and amongst whose buildings they must have occupied, if at all, a distinguished place. But, if not erected by Herod, there is then no period at which we can stop short of the Monarchy. So elaborate and costly a structure is inconceivable in the disturbed and impoverished state of the

The Enclosure.

---

[1] *Ant.* i. 14.   [2] *B. J.* iv. 9, § 7.
[3] For the later list of witnesses see Robinson's *B. R.* ii. 77, 78.

nation after the Return. It is to the kings, at least, that the walls must be referred, and, if so, to none so likely as one of the sovereigns to whom they are ascribed by Jewish and Mussulman [1] tradition, — David or Solomon. Beyond this we can hardly expect to find a continuous proof. But by this time, we have almost joined the earlier tradition implied in the reception of the Book of Genesis, with its detailed local description, into the Jewish Sacred Books.

With this early origin of the present enclosure its appearance [2] fully agrees. With the long continuity of the tradition agrees also the general character of Hebron and its vicinity. There is no spot in Palestine, except, perhaps, Mount Gerizim, where the *genius loci* has been so slightly disturbed in the lapse of centuries. There is already a savor of antiquity in the earliest mention of Hebron, "built seven years before Zoan [3] in Egypt." In it the names of the Amorite [4] inhabitants were preserved long after they had perished else-

---

[1] The Mussulman name at the present day for the enclosure is " the wall of Solomon."

[2] The peculiarities of the masonry are these: — (1.) Some of the stones are very large; Dr. Wilson mentions one 38 feet long, and 3 feet 4 inches deep; others are 16 feet long, and 5 feet high. The largest in the Haram wall at Jerusalem is 24½ feet. But yet (2) the surface, in splendid preservation, is very finely worked, more so than the finest of the stones at the south and southwest portion of the enclosure at Jerusalem; the sunken part round the edges (sometimes called the "bevel") very shallow, with no resemblance at all to mere "rustic work." (3.) The cross joints are not always vertical, but some are oblique. (4.) The wall is divided by pilasters about 2 feet 6 inches wide, and 5 feet apart, running the entire height of the ancient wall. There are eight of these pilasters at the ends, and sixteen at the sides of the enclosure. These observations are taken partly from Mr. Grove, who visited Hebron in 1859, partly from Dr. Robinson *B. R.* ii. 75, 76.) The length and breadth are given by Dr. Robinson respectively at 200 and 150 feet, by Signor Pierotti at 198½ and 113½ feet, who also makes the ancient wall 48 feet high, and 6½ feet thick.

[3] Num. xiii. 22.   [4] Jud. i. 10.

where; and from the time that the memory of Abraham first begun to be cherished there it seems never to have ceased. "The Terebinth, as old as the Creation,"[1] was shown in the time of Josephus. The Terebinth gave to the spot where it stood the name which lingers there down to the present day,[2] centuries after the tree itself has disappeared. The fair held beneath it, the worship offered, show that the Patriarch was regarded almost as a Divinity. The "oak of Abraham," now called "the oak (*Sindian*) of Sibteh," which stands in the valley of Eshcol, about a mile westward of Hebron, though not able to lay claim to the same antiquity as the long vanished Terebinth, yet seems to have divided the traditional honors with it. Josephus, who, in one of his works, speaks of the Terebinth, in another speaks of the oak, "the Ogygian," antediluvian oak,[3] and this is the view taken by the Septuagint. It is still in a green old age. Since I saw it in 1853, the glory of its spreading branches has been somewhat diminished; one large bough had fallen in 1856 to the terror, almost the awe, of the surrounding peasants; but the trunk[4] and the main limbs of

---

[1] *B. J.* iv. 9, § 7.

[2] The name "Terebinthus" was a recognized appellation of the spot in the time of Jerome. The field immediately northeast of the building called Rametel-Khalil, is known by the name of the "Halkath-el-Butm," "Field of the Terebinth."

[3] Joseph. *Ant.* i. 10, § 4, τὴν Ὠγύγην καλουμενὴν δρῦν.

[4] "In the winter of 1856-57, when in the streets of Jerusalem the snow fell deep and lay for many days, the accumulation upon the Abraham's oak was so great that one of the finest boughs gave way under the weight and fell to the ground. Owing to a superstition that any person who should cut or maim the oak would lose his first-born son, considerable difficulty was experienced in procuring hands to saw up the timber for transportation to Jerusalem. Seven camels were loaded with the wood of the one limb of this fine tree." A paper "On Three Oaks in Palestine,"

the tree remain vigorous and knotted and vast as before. Not seldom in our own churchyards the aged yew and the aged church stand side by side; and, as we glance from one to the other, we hardly know which of the two monuments of the past is the most venerable, the most affecting. Even so it is with "the oak of Abraham" and the sanctuary which we are now more especially considering.

With the sanctuary no less than with the oak, his name is indissolubly connected. Very early in the Middle Ages, that sepulchral quadrangle assumed the title of "the Castle of Abraham." But from thence the name spread to the whole place. The Mussulman name of " Elkhalîl," " The Friend (of God), has as completely superseded in the native population the Israelite name of "Hebron," as the name of "Hebron" had already superseded the Canaanite name of " Kirjath-arba." The town itself, which in ancient times must have been at some distance (as is implied in the original account of the purchase of the burial-place), from the sepulchre, has descended from the higher ground on which it was formerly situated, and clustered round the tomb which had become the chief centre of attraction. A similar instance may be noted in the name of El-Lazarieh, applied to Bethany, from the reputed tomb of Lazarus, round which the modern village has gathered. In our own country a parallel may be observed at St. Alban's. The town of Verulam has crossed the river from the northern bank on which it formerly stood, and has climbed the southern

by J. D. Hooker, M. D., in the Transactions of the Linnæan Society, vol. xxiii. p. 382. It contains (plate xxxvi.) an excellent representation of the oak, of which the scientific name is *Quercus pseudococcifera.*

hill in order to enclose the grave of S. Alban, whose name, in like manner, has entirely superseded that of the original Verulam.

For the sake of this sacred association, the town has become one of the Four Holy Places of Islam and of Judaism, — the other three in the sacred group being, in the case of Islam, Mecca, Medinah, and Jerusalem ; in the case of Judaism, Jerusalem, Safed, and Tiberias. The Mosque is said to have been founded and adorned in the successive reigns of Sultan Kelaoun, and of his son Naser-Mohammed, in the thirteenth and fourteenth centuries. Its property consists of some of the best land in the plains of Sharon and Philistia.

But of all the proofs of the sanctity of the place the most remarkable is the impenetrable mystery in which the sanctuary has been involved, being in fact a living witness of the unbroken local veneration with which the three religions of Jew, Christian, and Mussulman have honored the great Patriarch. The stones of the enclosure have, as has been said, been noticed from the time of Josephus downwards. The long roof of the Mosque, the upper part of its windows, the two minarets at the southwest and northeast corners rising above the earlier and later walls of the enclosure, have been long familiar to travellers. But what lay within had, till within the present year, been a matter if not of total ignorance, yet of uncertainty more provoking than ignorance itself. There were confused accounts[1] of an early Christian Church, of a subsequent mosque, of the cave and its situation, which

[1] Of these there is a collection in the Appendix to Quatremère's Translation of the History of the Mamelook Sultans of Egypt, published by the Oriental Translation Fund, vol. i. part ii. p. 230-242.

I.]   *VISIT OF THE PRINCE OF WALES.*   165

transpired through widely contradictory statements of occasional Jewish and Christian pilgrims, Antoninus, Arculf, and Sæwulf, Benjamin of Tudela, and Maundeville. For the six hundred years since the Mussulman occupation, in A.D. 1187, no European, except in disguise, was known to have set foot within the sacred precincts. Three accounts alone of such visits have been given in modern times; one, extremely brief and confused, by Giovanni Finati, an Italian servant of Mr. Bankes, who entered as a Mussulman;[1] a second, by an English clergyman, Mr. Monro, who, however, does not profess to speak from his own testimony;[2] a third, by far the most distinct, by the Spanish renegade Badia, or " Ali Bey."[3] While the other sacred places in Palestine, — the Mosque at Jerusalem, within the last ten years, the Mosque of Damascus, within the last two years, — have been thrown open, at least to distinguished travellers, the Mosque of Hebron still remained, even to royal personages, hermetically sealed.

To break through this mystery, to clear up this uncertainty, even irrespectively of the extraordinary interest attaching to the spot, was felt by those most concerned, to be an object not unworthy of the first visit of a Prince of Wales to the Holy Land.

From the moment that the expedition was definitively arranged in January 1862, it was determined by His Royal Highness and his advisers, that the attempt should be made, if it were found compatible with prudence, and with the

The visit of the Prince of Wales

---

[1] *Travels of Finati*, 1830, ii. 236.
[2] *Summer Ramble in Syria*, 1835, i. 242.
[3] *Travels of Ali Bey* (1803–1807), ii. 232.

respect due to the religious feelings of the native population. On arriving at Jerusalem, an inquiry immediately arose, as to the possibility of accomplishing this long-cherished design. Mr. Finn, then the English Consul, had already prepared the way, by requesting a Firman from the Porte for this purpose. The Government at Constantinople, aware of the susceptible fanaticism of the population of Hebron, sent, instead of a direct order, a Vizierial letter of recommendation to the Governor of Jerusalem, leaving in fact the whole matter to his discretion. The Governor, Sûraya Pasha, — partly from the natural difficulties of the proposed attempt, partly, it may be, from his own personal feeling on the subject, — held out long and strenuously against taking upon himself the responsibility of a step which had hitherto no precedent. Even as lately as the preceding year, he had resisted the earnest entreaty of a distinguished French scholar and antiquary, though armed with the recommendations of his own government and of Fuad Pasha, then Turkish Commissioner in Syria. The negotiation devolved on General Bruce, the Governor of the Prince of Wales, assisted by the interpreter of the party, Mr. Noel Moore, son of the Consul-General of Beyrût, and himself now the Consul at Jerusalem. It may truly be said, — as it was in enumerating the qualifications of the lamented General after his death, — that the tact and firmness which he showed on this occasion were worthy of the first ranks of diplomacy. Many grave political difficulties might, in other and grander spheres, have been unlocked by the dexterity with which he gained admittance to the Mosque of Hebron.

Sûraya Pasha offered every other civility or honor

that could be paid. The General took his position on the ground, that since the opening of the other Holy Places, this was the one honor left for the Turkish Government to award on the rare occasion of a visit of the Prince of Wales. He urged, too, the feeling with which the request was made; that we, as well as they, had a common interest in the Patriarchs common to both religions; and that nothing was claimed beyond what would be accorded to Mussulmans themselves. At last the Pasha appeared to give way. But a new alarm arose out of a visit of the Royal party to the shrine commonly called the Tomb of David, in Jerusalem.

The "Tomb of David," could it only be ascertained, would be of considerable importance, not only on account of its intrinsic interest, but because it would determine the disputed question of the site of Mount Zion and the City of David, in which the sepulchre was undoubtedly situated. And, if discovered at all, it would be capable of almost certain identification, because as containing the graves of by far the larger part of the Kings of Judah, it must be a sepulchral catacomb of considerable extent. The spot now shown as the site of the tomb is beneath the ancient church claimed by Christian tradition as the *Cœnaculum* or Upper Chamber of the Last Supper, of the Pentecostal assembly, of the death of the Virgin, and of the burial of Stephen. This spot is by the Mussulmans, — and apparently by them alone, — believed to be the tomb of David and his son Solomon. Their belief rests on too recent and too questionable a foundation to be of any substantial value;

and for this reason no special stress[1] was laid on the request that it should be made accessible to the Prince of Wales. But on our visit to the Chapel of the "Cœnaculum," which is shown to all travellers, there seemed to be no decided disinclination to permitting some approach to the chamber beneath. This accordingly we saw. It is evidently the crypt of the church above. At the east end of this chamber is a recess fenced off by an iron gate, through which is visible a cenotaph, such as is always found over the graves of Mussulman saints. It is a large coffin-like structure, covered with a green cloth, on which hangs the inscription,[2] "O David, whom God has made vicar, rule mankind in truth." Immediately in front of the shrine is a well. On the south side of the recess is a small window, and a wooden door. Over this door is an Arabic inscription, "This is the gate of the garden of Paradise," — which is the usual designation of a saint's tomb, — and the door, according to the keepers of the Mosque, leads to the cavern itself, but had never been opened as far back as the memory of themselves or their forefathers extended. It was to this door, which the Prince and a few members of his suite

[1] The "sepulchre of David" is mentioned by Nehemiah (iii. 16), as known after the return from the captivity; and in the Acts of the Apostles (ii. 29) and Josephus (*Ant.* vii. 15, 3; xiii. 8, 4; xvi. 7, 1,) at the time of the Christian era. The last authentic mention of it is in the time of Hadrian (*Dio Cassius*, lxix. 14). For the traditions respecting it see *Sinai and Palestine*, c. xiv. 455; Williams' *Holy City*, ii. 505-513.

[2] This recess is described and engraved, with some exaggeration, in the *City of the Great King* (p. 209), by the American Dr. Barclay, from the representation of Miss Barclay, who, by a fortunate accident, obtained admission. It is said that she gained such a celebrity from this sketch as to be known usually in her own country by the name of "the Daughter of Zion."

were allowed to approach closely, that our attention was chiefly attracted. But the keepers were resolute; the people in the neighborhood became excited; the excitement was increased by the number of Europeans who had been drawn to the spot by the natural curiosity of the occasion; and finally, the Pasha himself arrived with a troop of soldiers, inspired by a feeling, no doubt, similar to that which brought down Claudius Lysias from the fortress of Antonia to the court of the Temple, in the scene so forcibly described in the "Acts of the Apostles."[1] A long argument ensued, in which the whole question was discussed, together with the further and more important problem of the admission to the Mosque of Hebron. His arguments were extremely characteristic. "You did not order the pavement of the Chapel of the Holy Sepulchre to be taken up; yet if it be really a Jewish tomb, the Holy Sepulchre must be underneath." "When the tomb of the Prophet at Medinah needed repair, a rich recompense was offered to any one who would go in for the purpose. A man was found bold enough to make the attempt; he went in and repaired it; and on coming out was put to death. That was his recompense. This is our sentiment on the subject of opening the tombs of saints." "Even if this or the tomb of Hebron were open, I should not go in; I would not approach any one so holy as Abraham or David." "I will, if you wish, consult the Moollah or the Kadi; but I know beforehand what his answer will be."

The difficulties raised in this attempt naturally com-

[1] "Tidings came unto the chief captain of the band, that all Jerusalem was in an uproar: who immediately took soldiers and centurions, and ran down unto them."—Acts xxi. 31, 32.

plicated the question, in which the Prince was chiefly interested, of the access to Hebron; and in the course of that evening the Pasha finally declared that the responsibility was too grave, and that he could not undertake to guarantee the Prince's safety from the anger, either of the population of Hebron, or of the Patriarchs themselves, who were always on the watch within their tombs to avenge any injury or affront to their sanctity.[1]

It was an anxious moment. On the one hand, there was the doubt, now seriously raised, as to the personal safety of the attempt, which though it hardly entered into the Prince's own calculation, was a paramount question for those who were charged with the responsibility of the step. On the other hand the point, having been once raised, could not be lightly laid aside; the more so, as it was strongly felt that to allow of a refusal in the case of the Prince of Wales, would establish an impregnable precedent against future relaxations, and close the doors of the Mosque more firmly than ever against all inquirers. General Bruce adopted a course which ultimately proved successful. He announced to the Pacha the extreme displeasure of the Prince at the refusal, and declared his intention of leaving Jerusalem instantly for the Dead Sea; adding that if the sanctuary at Hebron could not be entered, the Prince would decline to visit Hebron altogether. We started immediately on a three days'

[1] An illustration of this occurred on my journey in 1853. In visiting the "Tomb of the Prophet (or Patriarch) Seth," on the Anti-Lebanon, one of our party was standing with his back towards the entrance. "Tell him," said the keeper of the mosque to our dragoman, "that he would not turn his back upon the Sultan: why should he not show at least equal respect to the Prophet?"

expedition, the usual excursion to Bethlehem, the Dead Sea, and Jericho. It will readily be supposed that in this route there is nothing to relate that is not familiar to every Eastern traveller or reader of Eastern travels. Only I may remark the extraor- <small>Bethlehem.</small> dinary effect produced by the beauty of the people of Bethlehem — of the children especially — often observed before, but not often seen to such advantage as then, when through every broken wall or ruined window of that rugged and narrow street, from every housetop that overhung our long cavalcade, every face in the village was looking down upon us, and every face (it is hardly too much to say) was beautiful. And another impression not less pleasing, even if accidental, was the " peace and good will " which seemed to prevail amongst the different religious communities Greek, Latin, Armenian, which cluster round the scene of the Nativity, contrasted with the jealousies and rivalries, Greek, Latin, Armenian, Protestant, which rage round the scene of the Sepulchre at Jerusalem, and which the visit of any distinguished personage only brings more clearly to light.

Out of the wide and wild sweep of hills round Bethlehem, which formed the cradle of the Psalms of David, we passed into the still wider and wilder sweep of the hills, over which he wandered in the years of his early manhood. These high upland regions are indeed the " wilderness of Judah " and, as we rode over their huge indulations, they were silent and desolate as the desert itself — till suddenly every barren ridge appeared bristling with groups of armed Arabs. For a few moments there was an expectation of attack. It is this incident which in foreign journals has been transformed into the story of the capture and release of the Prince of Wales. It was, in fact, the alarm which the streaming pennons and spears of our Turkish escort had struck into the Bedouin tribes, who, being in a state of chronic warfare with the government at Jerusalem, imagined that a hostile assault was intended. A few words from one of our party who rode forward to explain, dissolved the illusion, and the hills were in a moment as silent and as lifeless as before.

We descended upon the magnificent gorge of the convent of Mar Saba, and in a small platform in the gorge found our own tents pitched. But close beside was a smaller encampment, which contained Sûraya Pasha, — nominally, to secure the Prince's safe passage through the disturbed Arab tribes, but really to reopen the negotiations about Hebron. He had followed us by the more direct route from Jerusalem, and on that same evening sent a formal message offering to make the attempt, if the numbers were limited to the Prince and two or three of the suite, and promising to go himself to Hebron to prepare for the event.

<small>Return to Jerusalem.</small> This proposal was guardedly, but decisively accepted. The next day we still continued on our march to the Jordan; and the third day returned from Jericho to Jerusalem, up the well-known ascent of Adummin — the scene of the parable of the Good Samaritan,[1] and caught the view of the city from the memorable point on the road of our Lord's triumphal entry. The whole cavalcade halted at that long ledge of rock, where "He beheld the city and wept over it."[2] Before us lay the view, still splendid, of the

---

[1] See *Sinai and Palestine*, c. xiii. 424.   [2] *Ibid.* c. iii. 192.

APPROACH TO HEBRON.

Mosque of Omar, the Temple platform, the broken outline of Jerusalem, the deep ravine of the Kedron. Behind us lay Mount Olivet, its " stones,"[1] its " olive-trees," its " fig-trees,"[2] — even the flock of the black " goats " and white " sheep,"[3] which at that moment followed their shepherd over the slope of the hill,— all full of the Divine teaching, by which every portion of its rugged sides has been consecrated.

Our return was on the Saturday evening. On Sunday the Prince attended Divine Service in the English Church, and the rest of the day was quietly spent in Jerusalem. Early on the morning of Monday the 7th of April, we left our encampment, and moved in a southerly direction. The object of our journey was mentioned to no one. On our way we were joined by Dr. Rosen, the Prussian Consul at Jerusalem, well known to travellers in Palestine, from his profound knowledge of sacred geography, and in this instance, doubly valuable as a companion, from the special attention which he had paid to the topography of Hebron [4] and its neighborhood. Before our arrival at Hebron, the Pasha had made every preparation to insure the safety of the experiment. What he feared was, no doubt, a random shot or stone from some individual fanatic, who might have held his life cheap at the cost of avenging what he thought an outrage on the sancti-ties of his religion. Against Indian pilgrims, who are well known to hang about these sacred places, we had been especially warned, and one or two such we did in fact meet on our way and on our return. Accord-

[1] Luke xix. 40. [2] Matt. xxi. 19; xxiv. 32.
[3] Matt. xxv. 32.
[4] See his two Essays in the *Zeitschrift der Morgenländischen Gesellschaft*, xi. 50; xii. 489.

ingly, as the protracted file wound through the narrow valley by which the town of Hebron is approached, underneath the walls of those vineyards on the hillsides, which have made the vale of Eschol immortal, the whole road on either side for more than a mile was lined with soldiers. The native population, which usually, on the Prince's approach to a town, streamed out to meet him, was invisible, it may be from compulsion, it may be from silent indignation We at length reached the green sward in front of the town, crowned by the Quarantine and the Governor's residence. There Sûraya Pasha received us. It had been arranged, in accordance with the Pasha's limitation of the numbers, that His Royal Highness should be accompanied, besides the General, by the two members of the party who had given most attention to Biblical pursuits, so as to make it evident that the visit was not one of mere curiosity, but had also a distinct scientific purpose. It was, however, finally conceded by the Governor, that the whole of the suite should be included, amounting to seven persons besides the Prince. The servants remained behind. We started on foot, two and two, between two files of soldiers, by the ancient pool of Hebron, up the narrow streets of the modern town, still lined with soldiers. Hardly a face was visible as we passed through; only here and there a solitary guard, stationed at a vacant window, or on the flat roof of a projecting house, evidently to guarantee the safety of the party from any chance missile. It was, in fact, a complete military occupation of the town. At length we reached the southeastern corner of the massive wall of enclosure, the point at which inquiring travellers from generation to generation have been checked

The Approach.

in their approach to this, the most ancient and the most authentic of all the Holy Places of the Holy Land. "Here," said Dr. Rosen, "was the farthest limit of my researches." Up the steep flight of the exterior staircase, — gazing close at hand on the polished surface of the wall, amply justifying Josephus's account of the marble-like appearance of the huge stones which compose it, — we rapidly mounted. At the head of the staircase, which by its long ascent showed that the platform of the Mosque was on the uppermost slope of the hill, and therefore above the level where, if anywhere, the sacred cave would be found, a sharp turn at once brought us within the precincts, and revealed to us for the first time the wall from the inside. A later wall of Mussulman times has been built on the top of the Jewish enclosure. The enclosure itself, as seen from the inside, rises but a few feet above the platform.[1]

Here we were received with much ceremony by five or six persons, corresponding to the Dean and Canons of a Christian cathedral. They were the representatives of the Forty hereditary guardians of the Mosque. *The Entrance of the Mosque.*

We passed at once through an open court into the Mosque. With regard to the building itself, *The Mosque.* two points at once became apparent. First, it was clear that it had been originally a Byzantine church. To any one acquainted with the cathedral of S. Sophia at Constantinople, and with the monastic churches of Mount Athos, this is evident from the double narthex or portico, and from the four pillars

---

[1] The expression of Arculf (*Early Travellers*, p. 7), that the precinct was surrounded by a low wall (*humili muro*) might be explained if we suppose that he was speaking of it as seen from the inside.

of the nave. Secondly, it was clear that it had been converted at a much later period into a mosque. This is indicated by the pointed arches, and by the truncation of the apsis. The transformation was said by the guardians of the Mosque to have been made by Sultan Kelaoun. The whole building occupies (to speak roughly) one third of the platform. The windows are sufficiently high to be visible from without, above the top of the enclosing wall.

I now proceed to describe the Tombs of the Patriarchs, premising always that these tombs, like all those in Mussulman mosques, and indeed like most tombs in Christian churches, do not profess to be the actual places of sepulture, but are merely monuments or cenotaphs in honor of the dead who lie beneath. Each is enclosed within a separate chapel or shrine, closed with gates or railings similar to those which surround or enclose the private chapels or royal tombs in Westminster Abbey. The two first of these shrines or chapels are contained in the inner portico or narthex, before the entrance into the actual building of the Mosque. In the recess on the right is the shrine of Abraham, in the recess on the left that of Sarah, each guarded by silver gates.

The Shrine of Sarah. The shrine of Sarah we were requested not to enter, as being that of a woman. A pall lay over it. The shrine of Abraham, after a momentary *The Shrine of Abraham.* hesitation was thrown open. The guardians groaned aloud. But their chief turned to us with the remark, "The princes of any other nation should have passed over my dead body sooner than enter. But to the eldest son of the Queen of England we are willing to accord even this privilege."

I.] SHRINES OF ABRAHAM AND REBEKAH. 177

He stepped in before us, and offered an ejaculatory prayer to the dead Patriarch, "Oh, Friend of God, forgive this intrusion." We then entered. The chamber is cased in marble. The so-called tomb consists of a coffin-like structure, about six feet high, built up of plastered stone or marble, and hung with three carpets,[1] green embroidered with gold. They are said to have been presented by Mohamed II. the conqueror of Constantinople, Selim I. the conqueror of Egypt, and the late Sultan Abdul Mejid. Fictitious as the actual structure was, it was impossible not to feel a thrill of unusual emotion at standing on such a spot, — an emotion enhanced by the rare occasion which had opened the gates of that consecrated place, as the guardian of the Mosque kept repeating to us, as we stood round the tomb, "to no one less than the representative of England."

Within the area of the church or mosque were shown the tombs of Isaac and Rebekah. They are placed under separate chapels, in the walls of which are windows, and of which the gates are grated not with silver but iron bars. Their situation, planted as they are in the body of the Mosque, may indicate their Christian origin. In almost all Mussulman sanctuaries, the tombs of distinguished persons are placed, not in the centre of the building, but in the corners.[2] To Rebekah's tomb the same decorous rule of the exclusion of male visitors naturally applied as in the case of Sarah's. But on requesting to see the

<small>The Shrine of Rebekah.</small>

---

[1] In Ali Bey's time there were nine carpets. — *Travels*, ii. 233.

[2] The arrangement, however, described by Arculf is somewhat different. He speaks of the bodies (probably meaning the tombs) lying north and south, under slabs of stone. The tombs of the wives he also describes as apart, and of a meaner construction. — *Early Travellers*, p. 7.

tomb of Isaac, we were entreated not to enter; and on asking, with some surprise, why an objection which had been conceded for Abraham should be raised in the case of his far less eminent son, were answered that the difference lay in the characters of the two Patriarchs, — "Abraham was full of lovingkindness; he had withstood even the resolution of God against Sodom and Gomorrah; he was goodness itself, and would overlook any affront. But Isaac was proverbially jealous, and it was exceedingly dangerous to exasperate him. When Ibrahim Pasha (as conqueror of Palestine) had endeavored to enter, he had been driven out by Isaac, and fell back as if thunderstruck."

The Shrine of Isaac.

The chapel, in fact, contains nothing of interest; but I mention this story[1] both for the sake of the singular sentiment which it expresses, and also because it well illustrates the peculiar feeling which has tended to preserve the sanctity of the place, — an awe amounting to terror, of the great personages who lay beneath, and who would, it was supposed, be sensitive to any disrespect shown to their graves, and revenge it accordingly.

The shrines of Jacob and Leah were shown in recesses corresponding to those of Abraham and Sarah, — but in a separate cloister, opposite the entrance of the Mosque. Against Leah's tomb, as seen through the iron gate, two green banners reclined, the origin and meaning of which was unknown. They are placed in the pulpit on Fridays. The gates of Jacob's tomb were opened without difficulty, though with a deep groan from the bystanders. There was some good painted glass in one of the win-

The Shrine of Leah

The Shrine of Jacob.

[1] I have been unable to discover the origin of this legend.

dows. The structure was of the same kind as that in the shrine of Abraham, but with carpets of a coarser texture. Else it calls for no special remark.

Thus far the monuments of the Mosque adhere strictly to the Biblical account as given above. This is the more remarkable, because in these particulars the agreement is beyond what might have been expected in a Mussulman sanctuary. The prominence given to Isaac, whilst in entire accordance with the Sacred narrative, is against the tenor of Mussulman tradition, which exalts Ishmael into the first place. And, in like conformity with the Sacred narrative, but unlike what we should have expected, had mere fancy been allowed full play, is the exclusion of the famous Rachel, and the inclusion of the insignificant Leah.

The variation which follows rests, as I am informed by Dr. Rosen, on the general tradition of the country (justified, perhaps, by an ambiguous expression of Josephus [1]) that the body of Joseph, after having been deposited first at Shechem, was subsequently transported to Hebron. But the peculiar situation of this alleged tomb agrees with the exceptional

The Shrine of Joseph.

[1] "The bodies of the brothers of Joseph after a time were buried by their descendants in Hebron; but the bones of Joseph afterwards, when the Hebrews migrated from Egypt, were taken to Canaan." — *Ant.* ii. 8, 2. This may be intended merely to draw a distinction as to the time of removal, but probably it refers also to a difference in the places of burial, and expresses nothing positive on the subject. In Acts vii. 15, 16, the sons of Jacob are represented as all equally buried at Shechem; but then it is with the perplexing addition that they were buried in the same place as *Jacob*, and "in the sepulchre that *Abraham* bought for a sum of money from the sons of Emmor the father of Shechem." The burial of Joseph at Shechem is distinctly mentioned in Josh. xxiv. 32. "The bones of Joseph, which the children of Israel brought up out of Egypt, buried they *in Shechem*, in '*the parcel of the field*' which Jacob bought of the sons of Hamor the father of Shechem for a hundred pieces of silver; and it became the inheritance of the sons of Joseph."

character of the tradition. It is in a domed chamber attached to the enclosure from the outside, and reached, therefore, by an aperture[1] broken through the massive wall itself, and thus visible on the exterior of the southern side of the wall. It is less costly than the others, and it is remarkable that, although the name of his wife (according to the Mussulman version, Zuleika) is inserted in the certificates given to pilgrims who have visited the Mosque, no grave having that appellation is shown. A staff was hung up in a corner of the chamber. There were painted windows as in the shrine of Jacob. According to the story told by the guardian of the Mosque, Joseph was buried in the Nile, and Moses recovered the body, 1005 years afterwards, by marrying an Egyptian wife who knew the secret.

No other tombs were exhibited inside the Mosque. In a mosque on the northern side of the great Mosque were two shrines, resembling those of Isaac and Rebekah, which were afterwards explained to us as merely ornamental. On a platform immediately outside the Jewish wall on the north side, and seen from the hill rising immediately to the northeast of the Mosque, is the dome of a mosque named *Jawaliyeh*, said to have been built by the Emir Abou Said Sanjar Jâwali, from whom, of course, it derives its name, in the place of the tomb of Judas, or Judah, which he caused to be destroyed.[2]

The Mosque of Jâwali.

These are the only variations from the catalogue of tombs in the Book of Genesis. In the fourth century,

---

[1] This aperture was made by Dâhar Barkok, A. D. 1382–1389. — Quatremère, 247.

[2] A. D. 1319, 1320. — Quatremère, i. part ii. p. 248.

THE MOSQUE OF JÂWALI.

the Bourdeaux Pilgrim saw only the six great patriarchal shrines. But from the seventh century downwards, one or more lesser tombs seem to have been shown. Arculf speaks of the tomb of Adam,[1] "which is of meaner workmanship than the rest, and lies not far off from them at the farthest extremity to the north." If we might take this direction of the compass to be correct, he must mean either "the tomb of Judah" or one of the two in the northern mosque. This latter conjecture is confirmed by the statement of Maundeville that the tombs[2] of Adam and Eve were shown; which would thus correspond to these two. The tomb of Joseph is first distinctly mentioned by Sæwulf, who says that "the bones of Joseph were buried more humbly than the rest, as it were at the extremity of the castle."[3] Mr. Monro describes further "a tomb of Esau, under a small cupola, with eight or ten windows, excluded from lying with the rest of the Patriarchs."[4] Whether by this he meant the tomb of Joseph, or the tomb of Judah, is not clear. A Mussulman tomb of Esau was shown in the suburb of Hebron called *Sir*.[5]

The tomb of Abner is shown in the town, and the tomb of Jesse on the hill facing Hebron on the south.

[1] The tomb of Adam was shown as the "Fourth" of the "Four," who, with the three Patriarchs, were supposed to have given to Hebron the name of Kirjath-Arba, "the city of the Four." By a strange mistake which Jerome has perpetuated in the Vulgate translation, the word *Adam* in Joshua xxiv. 15, "a great *man* among the Anakims," has been taken by some of the Rabbis as a proper name. "Adam maximus ibi inter Enacim situs est."
[2] Maundeville (*Early Travellers*, p. 161).
[3] A. D. 1102 (*Early Travellers*, p. 45).
[4] *Summer Ramble*, i. 243.
[5] Quatremère, i. pt. ii. p. 319. Probably *Sirah*, the scene of the murder of Abner, 2 Sam. iii. 26.

But these have no connection with the Mosque, or the patriarchal burying-place.

We have now gone through all the shrines, whether of real or fictitious importance, which the Sanctuary includes. It will be seen that up to this point no mention has been made of the subject of the greatest interest, namely, the sacred cave itself, in which one at least of the patriarchal family may possibly still repose intact, — the embalmed body of Jacob. It may be well supposed that to this object our inquiries were throughout directed. One indication alone of the cavern beneath was visible. In the interior of the Mosque, at the corner of the shrine of Abraham, was a small circular hole, about eight inches across, of which one foot above the pavement was built of strong masonry, but of which the lower part, as far as we could see and feel, was of the living rock.[1] This cavity appeared to open into a dark space beneath, and that space (which the guardians of the Mosque believed to extend under the whole platform) can hardly be anything else than the ancient cavern of Machpelah. This was the only aperture which the guardians recognized. Once, they said, 2,500 years

The Sacred Cave.

---

[1] This hole was not shown to Ali Bey, perhaps as being only an ordinary pilgrim. It is thus described by Mr. Monro or his informant: — " A baldachin, supported on four small columns over an octagon figure of black and white inlaid, round a small hole in the pavement" (i. 264). It is also mentioned by the Arab historians. " There is a vault that passes for the burial-place of Abraham, in which is a lamp always lighted. Hence the common expression among the people, ' the Lord of the *vault* and the *lamp*' " (Quatremère, i. pt. ii. p. 247). " Near the tomb of Abraham is a vault, where is a small gate leading to the *minbar* (pulpit). Into this hole once fell an idiot, who was followed by the servants of the Mosque. They saw a stone staircase of fifteen steps, which led to the *minbar*' (*Ibid.*). The lamp is also mentioned by Mr. Monro (i. p. 244), and by Benjamin of Tudela (see *infra*, p. 185).

ago, a servant of a great king had penetrated through some other entrance. He descended in full possession of his faculties, and of remarkable corpulence; he returned blind, deaf, withered, and crippled. Since then the entrance was closed, and this aperture alone was left, partly for the sake of allowing the holy air of the cave to escape into the Mosque, and be scented by the faithful; partly for the sake of allowing a lamp to be let down by a chain which we saw suspended at the mouth, to burn upon the sacred grave. We asked whether it could not be lighted now? "No," they said; "the saint likes to have a lamp at night, but not in the full daylight."

With that glimpse into the dark void we and the world without must for the present be satisfied. Whether any other entrance is known to the Mussulmans themselves, must be a matter of doubt. The original entrance to the cave, if it is now to be found at all, must probably be on the southern face of the hill, between the Mosque and the gallery containing the shrine of Joseph, and entirely obstructed by the ancient Jewish wall, probably built across it for this very purpose.

It seems to our notions almost incredible that Christians and Mussulmans, each for a period of 600 years, should have held possession of the sanctuary, and not had the curiosity to explore what to us is the one object of interest, — the cave. But the fact is undoubted that no account exists of any such attempt. Such a silence can only be explained (but it is probably a sufficient explanation) by the indifference which prevailed, throughout the Middle Ages, to any historical spots however interesting, unless they were actually consecrated as places of pilgrimage. The Mount of Olives, the site of the Temple of Solomon, the Rock of the Holy Sepulchre itself, were not thought worthy of even momentary consideration, in comparison with the chapels and stations which were the recognized objects of devotion. Thus at Hebron a visit to the shrines, both for Christians and Mussulmans, procures a certificate. The cave had therefore no further value. In the case of the Mussulmans this indifference is still more general. Sûraya Pasha himself, a man of considerable intelligence, professed that he had never thought of visiting the Mosque of Hebron for any other purpose than that of snuffing the sacred air, and he had never, till we arrived at Jerusalem, seen the wonderful convent of Mar Saba, or the Dead Sea, or the Jordan. And to this must be added, if not in his case, in that of Mussulmans generally, the terror which they entertain of the effect of the wrath of the Patriarchs on any one who should intrude into the place where they are supposed still to be in a kind of suspended animation. As far back as the seventeenth century it was firmly believed that if any Mussulman entered the cavern, immediate death would be the consequence.[1]

It should be mentioned, however, that two accounts are reported of travellers having obtained a nearer view of the cave than was accomplished in the visit of the Prince of Wales.

The first is contained in the pilgrimage of Benjamin of Tudela, the Jewish traveller of the twelfth century:—" The Gentiles have erected six sepulchres in this place, which they pretend to be those of Abraham

[1] Quaresmius, ii. 772.

and Sarah, Isaac and Rebekah, Jacob and Leah. The pilgrims are told that they are the sepulchres of the fathers, and money is extorted from them. But if any Jew comes, who gives an additional fee to the keeper of the cave, an iron door is opened, which dates from the time of our forefathers who rest in peace, and with a burning candle in his hands, the visitor descends into a first cave, which is empty, traverses a second in the same state, and at last reaches a third, which contains six sepulchres, those of Abraham, Isaac, and Jacob, and of Sarah, Rebekah, and Leah, one opposite the other. All these sepulchres bear inscriptions, the letters being engraved. Thus, upon that of Abraham we read, — 'This is the sepulchre of our father Abraham; upon whom be peace,' and so on that of Isaac, and upon all the other sepulchres. A lamp burns in the cave and upon the sepulchres continually, both night and day, and you there see tombs filled with the bones of Israelites, — for unto this day it is a custom of the house of Israel to bring hither the bones of their saints and of their forefathers, and to leave them there."

In this account,[1] which, as may be observed, does not profess to describe Benjamin's own experience, there are two circumstances (besides its general improbability) which throw considerable doubt on its accuracy. One is the mention of inscriptions, and of an iron door, which, as is well known, are never found in Jewish sepulchres. The other is the mention of the

[1] A somewhat similar account is given by Moawiych Ishmail, Prince of Aleppo,—that in A. D. 1089 the tombs of Abraham, Isaac, and Jacob were found; that many persons saw the bodies, preserved without change, and that in the cavern were arranged lamps of gold and silver (Quatremère, 245).

practice of Jews sending their bones to be buried in a place, which, as is evident from the rest of the narrative, could only be entered with the greatest difficulty.

The second account is that of M. Ermete Pierotti, who, having been an engineer in the Sardinian army, acted for some years as architect and engineer to Sûraya Pasha, at Jerusalem, and thus obtained, both in that city and at Hebron, access to places otherwise closed to Europeans. The following account appeared in the "Times" of April 30, 1862, immediately following on the announcement of the Prince's visit: —

<small>M. Ermete Pierotti.</small>

"The true entrance to the Patriarchs' tomb is to be seen close to the western wall of the enclosure, and near the northwest corner; it is guarded by a very thick iron railing, and I was not allowed to go near it. I observed that the Mussulmans themselves did not go very near it. In the court opposite the entrance-gate of the Mosque, there is an opening, through which I was allowed to go down for three steps, and I was able to ascertain by sight and touch that the rock exists there, and to conclude it to be about five feet thick. From the short observations I could make during my brief descent, as also from the consideration of the east wall of the Mosque, and the little information I extracted from the Chief Santon, who jealously guards the sanctuary, I consider that a part of the grotto exists under the Mosque, and that the other part is under the court, but at a lower level than that lying under the Mosque. This latter must be separated from the former by a vertical stratum of rock which contains an opening, as I conclude, for two reasons: first, because the east wall being entirely solid and massive, requires a good foundation; secondly, because the petitions which the Mussulmans present to the Santon to be transmitted to the Patriarchs are thrown, some through one opening, some through the other, according to the Patriarch to whom they are directed; and the Santon goes down by the way I went, whence I suppose that on that side there is a vestibule, and that the tombs may be found below it. I explained my conjectures to the Santon himself after leaving the Mosque, and he showed himself very much surprised at the time, and told the Pacha afterwards that I knew more about it than the Turks themselves. The fact is, that even the Pacha who governs the province has no right to penetrate into the sacred enclosure, where (according to the Mussulman legend) the Patriarchs are living, and only condescend to receive the petitions addressed to them by mortals."[1]

This statement of the entrance of the Santon, or Sheik of the Mosque, into the cave, agrees with the account which was given to me at Hebron in 1852; " that the cave consists of two compartments, into one of which a dervish or sheik is allowed to penetrate on special emergencies." Against this must be set the repeated assertions of the guardian of the Mosque, and of the Governor of Jerusalem, (which, as has been seen, are substantially confirmed by the Arab historians,) that no Mussulman has ever entered the cave within the memory of man Of the staircase

[1] M. Pierotti adds (what has often been observed before) that " the Jews who dwell in Hebron, or visit it, are allowed to kiss and touch a piece of the sacred rock close to the northwest corner, which they can reach through a small aperture. To accomplish this operation they are obliged to lie flat on the ground, because the aperture is on the ground level." This, however, is merely an access to the rock, not to the cave.

and gate described by M. Pierotti, there was no appearance on our visit, though we must have walked over the very spot, — being, in fact, the pavement in front of the Mosque. Of the separate apertures for throwing down the petitions we also saw nothing. And it would seem from Finati's account,[1] that the one hole down which he threw his petition was that by the tomb of Abraham.

The result of the Prince's visit will have been disappointing to those who expected a more direct solution of the mysteries of Hebron. But it has not been without its indirect benefits. In the first place, by the entrance of the Prince of Wales, the first step has been taken for the removal of the bar of exclusion from this most sacred and interesting spot. The relaxation may in future times be slight and gradual, and the advantage gained must be used with every caution; but it is impossible not to feel that some effect will be produced even on the devotees of Hebron when they feel that the Patriarchs have not suffered any injury or affront, and that even Isaac rests tranquilly in his grave.[2] And Englishmen may fairly rejoice that this advance in the cause of religious tolerance (if it may so be called) and of Biblical knowledge, was attained in the person of

Results of the Prince's visit.

---

[1] "I went into a mosque at Hebron and threw a paper down into a hole that is considered to be the tomb of Abraham, and according as the paper lodges by the way, or reaches the bottom, it is looked upon as a sign of good or ill-luck for the petitioner." — *Travels of Finati,* ii. p. 236.

[2] An account appeared in a French journal (*L'Ami de la Religion,* in May, 1862,) of the visit of the Prince of Wales to Hebron. Amidst curious smaller inaccuracies it gave a tolerably correct narrative of the transaction itself. The population of Hebron were, it was there stated, firmly convinced that some great disaster would befall Sûraya Pasha within the year.

the heir to the English throne, out of regard to the position which he and his country hold in the Eastern world.

In the second place, the visit has enabled us to form a much clearer judgment of the value of the previous accounts, to correct their deficiencies and to rectify their confusion. The narrative of Ali Bey, in particular, is now substantially corroborated. The existence and the exact situation of the cave underneath the floor of the Mosque, the appearance of the ancient enclosure from within, the precise relation of the different shrines to each other, and the general conformity of the traditions of the Mosque to the accounts of the Bible and of early travellers, are now for the first time clearly ascertained. To discover the entrance of the cave, to examine the actual places of the patriarchal sepulture, and to set (eyes if so be) on the embalmed body of Jacob, the only patriarch the preservation of whose remains is thus described,— must be reserved for the explorers of another generation, for whom this visit will have been the best preparation.

Meanwhile, it may be worth while to recall the general instruction furnished by the nearer contemplation of this remarkable spot. The narrative itself to which it takes us back stands alone in the Patriarchal history for the precision with which both locality and character are delineated. First, there is the death of Sarah in the city of Kirjath-Arba, whilst Abraham is absent,[1] apparently at Mamre. He comes to make the grand display of funeral grief, "mourning aloud and weeping aloud," such as would

General results.

[1] Gen. xxiii. 2.

befit so great a death. He is filled with the desire, not Egyptian, not Christian, hardly Greek or Roman, but certainly Jewish, to thrust away the dark shadow, that has fallen upon him, " to bury [1] his dead out of his sight." Then ensues the conference in the gate,— the Oriental place of assembly,[2] where the negotiators and the witnesses of the transaction, as at the present day, are gathered from the many comers and goers through " the gate of the city." As in the Gentile traditions of Damascus, and as in the ancient narrative of the pursuit of the five kings, Abraham is saluted by the native inhabitants, not merely as a wandering shepherd, but as a " Prince of God."[3] The inhabitants are, as we might expect, not the Amorites, but the Hittites, whose name is that recognized by all the surrounding nations. They offer him the most sacred of their sepulchres for the cherished remains.[4] The Patriarch maintains his determination to remain aloof from the Canaanite population, at the same time that he preserves every form of courtesy and friendliness, in accordance with the magnificent toleration and inborn gentleness which pervade his character. First, as in the attitude of Oriental respect, " he stands," and then, twice over, he prostrates himself on the ground, before the heathen masters of the soil.[5] Ephron, the son of Zohar, is worthy of the occasion; his courtesy matches that of the Patriarch himself:— " The field *give* I thee, the cave . . . . *give* I thee; in the presence of the sons of my people *give* I it thee." " What is that betwixt thee and me?"[6] It is precisely the pro-

---

[1] Gen. xxiii. 4.
[2] *Ibid.* 10.
[3] *Ibid.* 6.
[4] *Ibid.* 6.
[5] *Ibid.* 7-12.
[6] *Ibid.* 13-15.

fuse liberality[1] with which the Arab of the present time places everything in his possession at the disposal of the stranger. But the Patriarch, with the high independence of his natural character (shall we say, also, with the caution of his Jewish descendants?) will not be satisfied without a regular bargain. He "weighs out"[2] the coin. He specifies every detail in the property; not the field only, but the cave in the field, and the trees[3] in the field, and on the edge of the field, "were made sure." The result is the first legal contract recorded in human history, the first known interment of the dead, the first assignment of property to the Hebrew people in the Holy Land.[4]

To this graphic and natural scene, not indeed by an absolute continuity of proof, but by such evidence as has been given above, the cave of Machpelah carries us back. And if in the long interval which elapses between the description of the spot in the Book of Genesis (whatever date we assign to that description) and the notice of the present sanctuary by Josephus, so venerable a place and so remarkable a transaction are passed over without a word of recognition, this must, on any hypothesis, be reckoned amongst the many proofs that, in ancient literature, no argument can be drawn against a fact from the mere silence of authors, whether sacred or secular, whose minds were fixed on other subjects, and who were writing with another intention.

[1] Such exactly was the language of Aghyle Aga, as described in the 3d of these Notices.
[2] Gen. xxiii. 16.   [3] *Ibid.* 17.
[4] Several of the above details are suggested by an excellent passage on this subject in Thomson's *Land and Book*, p. 577-579.

We remained at Hebron for that day and during the following morning. It had been our original intention to have left the place immediately after our departure from the Mosque, and encamped at some distance from the town. But Dr. Rosen predicted beforehand that, if the entrance were once made, no additional precautions would be required. " They will be so awe-struck," he said, " at the success of your attempt, that they will at once acquiesce in the fact." And so it proved. Although we were still accompanied by a small escort, the rigid vigilance of the previous day was relaxed, and no indications appeared of any anger or vengeance.

In the early morning I visited, in company with Dr. Rosen, some of the remains of antiquity on the wooded hill facing the town of Hebron on the south. An ancient well on the slope of the hill is sometimes called " the Spring of Abraham," sometimes " the New Spring " *Ain-el-Jedidi ;* [1] this last title, as often the case in local designations, indicating rather the antiquity than the novelty of the place in question. It is vaulted over with masonry, and the channel, when not filled with water, is believed in the neighborhood to reach to the Mosque. In this vault the local tradition (attaching itself to the curious mistake before noticed, respecting the connection of "Adam " with Hebron) represents that Adam and Eve hid themselves after their flight from Paradise.[2] Somewhat

---

[1] Thus "New College," at Oxford, was called "New" in relation to its first appearance, and has retained its name though twelve other new colleges have arisen since.

[2] It was shown as such to Maundeville (*Early Travellers in Palestine*, p. 16).

higher up the hill is a ruin called *Deir Arbain*, (the Convent of the Forty Martyrs,) consisting of old masonry, which Dr. Rosen conjectures to be the remains of the fortress built at Hebron by Rehoboam.[1] In a corner of this building is the so-called tomb of Jesse.

After surveying the exterior of the Mosque, we rode over the hills, south of Hebron, to visit the probable scene of the romantic transaction, recorded in the Book of Joshua and the Book of Judges, between Caleb and his daughter Achsah.[2] A wide valley, unusually green, amidst the barren hills of the " south country," suddenly breaks down into an almost precipitous and still greener ravine. On the south side of this ravine is a village called *Dura*, possibly the *Adoraim* of the Book of Chronicles;[3] on the north, at the summit of a steeper and more rugged ascent, is *Dewir Dan*, which recalls the name of *Debir*, the fortress which Othniel stormed on the condition of winning Achsah for his bride. — " Give me," she said to her father, as she rode on her ass beside him, " a field," — " a blessing," — a rich field, such as that which lies spread in the green basin, which she and Caleb would first encounter in their ride from Hebron. " For thou hast given me a south land," — these dry rocky hills which extend as far as the eye can reach, till they melt into the hazy platform of the desert. " Give me also the 'bubblings' (*gulloth*) of water — the upper and the lower bubblings." It is an expressive word which seems to be used for " tumbling, falling waves," and is thus

[1] 1 Chron. xi. 10.
[2] Joshua xv. 16-19; Judges i. 11-15. See *Lectures on the Jewish Church*, p. 293, (Amer. ed.)
[3] 2 Chron. xi. 9.

especially applicable to the rare sight of the clear rivulet that, rising in the green meadow above mentioned, (*Ain Nunkar*,) falls and flows continuously down to the bottom of the ravine, and by its upper and nether streams gives verdure to the whole. The identification is not perhaps absolutely certain. But the scene lends itself to the incident in every particular.

We returned by many a vestige of ancient habitations, chiefly the ancient wells and cisterns, and the winepresses hewn out of the living rock,— consisting of the reservoir for the pressing of the grapes, the channel through which the juice was to run off, and the cellar or cavity into which it was to fall. The wide extent of view and the number of traditional or historical localities included in the prospect, gave to this investigation of the neighborhood of Hebron, and to our descent from its high elevation towards Jerusalem, an interest which equalled that with which I had traversed (in part) the same route on my first entrance into the Holy Land in 1853. The advantage of an intelligent guide, like Dr. Rosen, to whom every spot was familiar, both in its ancient and modern aspects, rendered the journey doubly instructive. On the nearer hills we explored in detail the remains [1] of the "House or High Place of Abraham," Ramet-el-khalil, the vestiges of the Temple, where the Patriarch had been almost worshipped by the Arabs as a divinity, and of the Oratory which Constantine had ordered to be erected, when at the Emperor's orders the sacred terebinth had been cut down, whence, as before re-

---

[1] The local tradition is that these ruins are the foundations of the Mosque of Hebron, before the builders were directed by a celestial light to the present site.

I.] *THE NEIGHBORHOOD OF HEBRON.* 195

marked, the name still lingers in the adjacent field. On a conical hill close by, — possibly called from this incident *Gebel-el-Batrak, the hill of the Patriarch,* — is the traditional site of the vision in which Abraham received the promise.[1] The wide horizon — the sea visible in the western distance — the traces of antique civilization all around, all so well according with the destinies of his race — would entitle the prospect, if the tradition had better ground, to be ranked with those views which, as I have elsewhere [2] observed, form such remarkable links between the history and the geography of the Chosen People. In the yet further distance to the northeast, a church or mosque on a hilltop deserves, at least, a momentary glance as the traditional tomb of the Prophet Gad or Nathan; if authentic, or even if only fanciful, how appropriately planted in the midst of those early scenes of David's life, in which those two Prophets played so large a part! From the hills to the westward, the plain of Philistia lay flat beneath us; and, as we advanced through their many undulations, we passed the ruins of the oratory which had stood on what the tradition of the fourth century marked out with considerable probability as the scene of Philip's encounter with the Ethiopian chamberlain [3] at the well by the roadside, almost directly at the point where through a wide valley opens what is still the usual route to Gaza — and (at least as compared with the northern road) " deserted " of villages. By the pools of Solomon, the

[1] Gen. xv. 1.
[2] *Sinai and Palestine,* c. ii. 130.
[3] Acts viii. 36. The remains of the Roman road and of a Roman milestone are still visible.

green vale of Urtas, the Latin convent of Beit Jala,[1] the Greek convent of the Cross, we returned to Jerusalem on the 5th of April, and left it on the following day for Bethel, Shiloh, and Nablûs.

[1] This convent, which overhangs the ridge of Bethlehem, is now usually identified with Zelah or Zelzah, the burial-place of the house of Saul (2 Sam. xxi. 14). It is a curious instance of the random guesses of the Monastic establishments, that the monks in the convent represented it to us as the site of Gideon's threshing-floor (Judg. vi. 11), which must, beyond question, have been three days' journey distant amongst the hills of Manasseh.

THE SAMARITAN PASSOVER.

PLAN OF MOUNT GERIZIM.

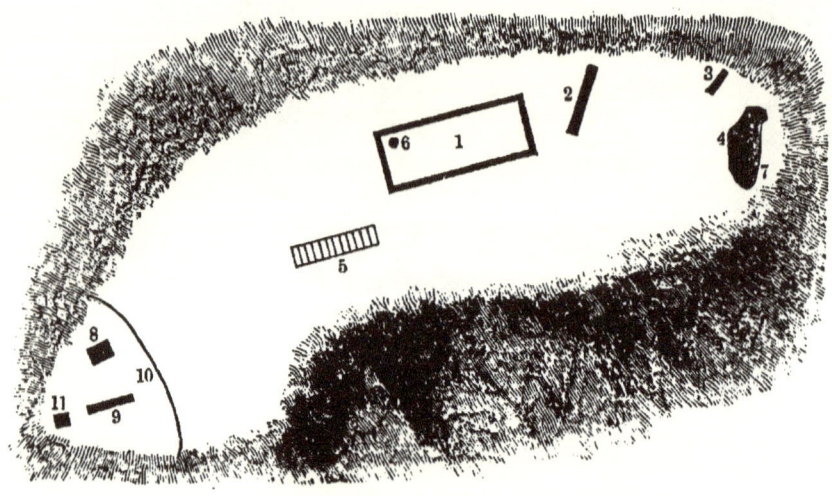

1. Fortress.
2. Seven steps of Adam out of Paradise.
3. Scene of the offering of Isaac, — a trough like that used for the Paschal Feast.
4. "Holy Place."
5. Joshua's Twelve Stones.
6. "Tomb of Sheik Ghranem," or "Shechem ben Hamor."
7. "Cave where the Tabernacle was built."
8. Hole where the Paschal sheep are roasted
9. Trench where they are eaten.
10. Platform for the celebration of the Passover.
11. Hole where the water is boiled.

II. THE SAMARITAN PASSOVER.

IF of all the Holy Places in Palestine the Mosque of Hebron was the one which, after my first journey, I most regretted to have left unseen amongst the sacred spectacles, the same may be said of the Samaritan Passover. This on the present occasion we were enabled to witness. A brief description of it had been already given to me in 1854 by Mr. Rogers,[1] now Consul at Damascus. I am induced to give a full account of its celebration as we saw it in 1862, not only from its intrinsic interest, but because it is evident that the ceremonial has been considerably modified since the time when it was first described to me. Even to that lonely community the influences of Western change have extended; and this is perhaps the last generation which will have the opportunity of witnessing this vestige of the earliest Jewish ritual.

The Samaritan Passover is celebrated at the same time as the Jewish — namely, on the full moon of the month Nisan. In the present instance, either by design or by a fortunate mistake, the Samaritan community had anticipated the 14th of the month by two days. It was on the evening of Saturday the 13th of April that we ascended Mount Gerizim, and visited the various traditional localities on the rocky platform which crowns the most ancient of sanctuaries. The

[1] His account has since been printed in his sister's interesting work, *Domestic Life in Palestine*, 281.

whole community — amounting, it is said, to one hundred and fifty-two, from which hardly any variation has taken place within the memory of man — were encamped in tents on a level space, a few hundred yards below the actual summit of the mountain,[1] selected on account of its comparative shelter and seclusion. The women[2] were shut up in the tents. The men were assembled on the rocky terrace in sacred costume. In 1854 they all wore the sacred costume. On this occasion most of them were in their ordinary dress. Only about fifteen of the elder men, amongst whom was the Priest Amram,[3] were clothed, as formerly was the case with the whole community, in long, white robes. To these must be added six youths,[4] dressed in white

The preparation.

[1] It is only within the last twenty years that the Samaritans (chiefly through the intervention of the English Consul) have regained the right, or rather the safety, of holding their festival on Mount Gerizim. For a long time before, they had celebrated the Passover like the modern Jews, and, as in the first celebration of the institution in Egypt, in their own houses. The performance of the solemnity on Gerizim is in strict conformity with the principle laid down in Deut. xvi 15: — "Thou shalt keep a solemn feast in the place which the Lord thy God shall choose," — and with the practice which prevailed in Judæa till the fall of Jerusalem, of celebrating the Passover at the Temple.

[2] Those women, who, by the approach of childbirth or other ceremonial reasons, were prevented from sharing in the celebration, remained in Nablûs.

[3] It is stated in Miss Rogers' *Domestic Life in Palestine* (249) that Amram is not properly a priest (the legitimate high priest, — the last descendant, as they allege, of Aaron, — having expired some years ago), and that he is only a Levite. He is, however, certainly called "the priest" (Cohen). He has two wives. The children of the first died in infancy, and he was therefore entitled, by Samaritan usage, to take a second. By her he has a son, Isaac. But, according to the Oriental law of succession, he will be succeeded in his office by his nephew Jacob, as the oldest of the family.

[4] These youths were evidently trained for the purpose; but whether they held any sacred office, I could not learn. In the Jewish ritual, the lambs were usually slain by the householders, but on great occasions (2 Chron. xxxv. 10) apparently by the Levites.

shirts and white drawers. The feet both of these and of the elders were at this time of the solemnity bare. It was about half an hour before sunset, that the whole male community in an irregular form (those attired as has been described in a more regular order) gathered round a long trough that had been previously dug in the ground; and the Priest, ascending a large rough stone in front of the congregation, recited in a loud chant or scream, in which the others joined, prayers or praises chiefly turning on the glories of Abraham and Isaac. Their attitude was that of all Orientals in prayer; standing, occasionally diversified by the stretching out of the hands, and more rarely by kneeling or crouching, with their faces wrapt in their clothes and bent to the ground,[1] towards the Holy Place on the summit of Gerizim. The Priest recited his prayers by heart; the others had mostly books, in Hebrew and Arabic.

Presently, suddenly, there appeared amongst the worshippers six sheep,[2] driven up by the side of the youths before mentioned. The unconscious innocence with which they wandered to and fro amongst the bystanders, and the simplicity in aspect and manner of the young men who tended them, more recalled a scene in Arcadia, or one of those inimitable patriarchal *tableaux* represented in the Ammergau Mystery, than a religious ceremonial. It did in fact faithfully recall the pastoral condition of the Israelites, when they emerged from the land of Goshen; when from their shepherds' flocks a lamb[3] or a kid was their only and their most suitable offering. The sun, mean-

The Sacrifice.

---

[1] Compare the attitude of Elijah (1 Kings xviii. 42; xix. 13).
[2] *Seven* sheep is the usual number. — *Domestic Life in Palestine*, 250.
[3] Ex. xii. 5. "Ye shall take it out from the sheep, or from the goats."

while, which hitherto had burnished up the Mediterranean in the distance, now sank very nearly to the farthest western ridge overhanging the plain of Sharon. The recitation became more vehement. The Priest turned about, facing his brethren, and the whole history of the Exodus, from the beginning of the Plagues of Egypt was rapidly, almost furiously, chanted. The sheep, still innocently playful, were driven more closely together. The setting sun [1] now touched the ridge. The youths burst into a wild murmur of their own, drew forth their long bright knives, and brandished them aloft. In a moment, the sheep were thrown on their backs, and the flashing knives rapidly drawn across their throats. Then a few convulsive but silent struggles, — "as a sheep — dumb — that openeth not his mouth," — and the six forms lay lifeless on the ground, the blood streaming from them; the one only Jewish sacrifice lingering in the world. In the blood the young men dipped their fingers, and a small spot was marked on the foreheads and noses of the children. A few years ago the red stain was placed on all. But this had now dwindled away into the present practice, preserved, we were told, as a relic or emblem of the whole. Then, as if in congratulation at the completion of the ceremony, they all kissed each other, in the Oriental fashion, on each side of the head.[2]

[1] "The whole assembly shall kill it 'between the two evenings'" (Ex. xii. 6). "Thou shalt sacrifice the Passover at evening, at the going down of the sun," (Deut. xvi. 6).

[2] I have recently seen an account of the Samaritan Passover, as celebrated in 1854, in Professor Petermann's Travels. He adds a few curious details, as for example, that, at the moment of the slaughter of the sheep, the High Priest recites in a loud voice the words from Exod. xii. 6: "And the whole assembly of the congregation of the children of Israel shall kill it in the evening."

The next process was that of the fleecing[1] and roasting of the slaughtered animals, for which the ancient Temple furnished such ample provisions. On the mountain-side two holes had been dug, one at some distance, of considerable depth, the other, close to the scene of the Sacrifice, comparatively shallow. In this latter cavity, after a short prayer, a fire was kindled, out of a mass of dry heath, juniper, and briers, such as furnish the materials for the conflagration in Jotham's Parable, delivered not far from this very spot. Over the fire were placed two caldrons full of water. Whilst the water boiled, the congregation again stood round, and (as if for economy of time) continued the recitation of the Book of Exodus, and bitter herbs were handed round wrapped in a strip of unleavened bread: " with unleavened bread and with bitter herbs shall they eat it."[2] Then was chanted another short prayer. After which the six youths again appeared, poured the boiling water over the sheep, and plucked off their fleeces. The right fore-legs[3] of the sheep, with the entrails, were thrown aside and burnt. The liver was carefully put back. Long poles were brought, on which the animals were spitted; near the bottom of each pole was a transverse peg or stick, to prevent the body from slipping off. As no part of the body is transfixed by this cross-stake, — as, indeed, the body hardly impinges on it at all, — there is at present but a very slight resemblance to a cruci-

---

[1] In the ancient Jewish ritual the lambs were skinned, as in western countries (2 Chron. xxxv. 11; Mishna, *Pesachim*, ch. v. 9). The process, as above described, was like that of our mode of taking off the hair from pigs after they have been killed.
[2] Ex. xii. 8.
[3] The right shoulder and the hamstrings (*Domestic Life in Palestine*, 250).

fixion. But it is possible that in earlier times the legs of the animal may have been attached to the transverse beam. So at least the Jewish rite is described by Justin Martyr, — " The Paschal Lamb, that is to be roasted, is roasted in a form like to that of the Cross. For one spit is thrust through the animal from head to tail, and another through its breast, to which[1] its forefeet are attached." He naturally saw in it a likeness of the Crucifixion. But his remark, under any view, is interesting: first, because, being a native of Nablûs, he probably drew his notices of the Passover from this very celebration ; which, as it would thus appear, has, even in this minute particular, been but very slightly modified since he saw it in the second century ; and, also, because, as he draws no distinction between this rite and that of the Jews in general, we have a right to infer that the Samaritan Passover is on the whole a faithful representation of the Jewish. That the spit was run right through the body of the animal in the Jewish ritual, and was of wood, as in the Samaritan, is clear from the account in the Mishna.[2]

The sheep were then carried to the other hole already mentioned, which was constructed in the form of the usual oven (*tannûr*) of Arab villages, — a deep circular pit sunk in the earth, with a fire kindled at the bottom. Into this the sheep were thrust down (it is said, but this I could not see), with care, to prevent the bodies from impinging on the sides,

The roasting.

---

[1] *Dial. cum Tryph.* c. 40.
[2] *Pesachim*, ch. vi. 7. It was to be wood, not iron, in order that the roasting might be entirely "by fire," and not by the hot iron: and the wood was to be pomegranate, as not emitting any water, and so not interfering with the roasting. Whether the spits on Gerizim were of pomegranate I did not observe.

and so being roasted by anything but the fire.[1] A hurdle was then put over the mouth of the pit, well covered with wet earth, so as to seal up the oven till the roasting was completed. "They shall[2] eat the flesh in that night roast with fire. Eat not of it raw, nor sodden at all with water, but roast with fire."

The ceremonial up to this time occupied about two hours. It was now quite dark, and the greater part of the community and of our company retired to rest. Five hours or more elapsed in silence, and it was not till after midnight that the announcement was made, that the feast was about to begin. The Paschal moon was still bright and high in the heavens. The whole male community was gathered round the mouth of the oven, and with reluctance allowed the intrusion of any stranger to a close inspection; a reluctance which was kept up during the whole of this part of the transaction, and contrasted with the freedom with which we had been allowed to be present at the earlier stages of the ceremony. It seemed as if the rigid exclusiveness of the ancient Paschal ordinance here came into play, — "A foreigner[3] shall not eat thereof; no uncircumcised person shall eat thereof."

Suddenly the covering of the hole was torn off, and up rose into the still moonlit sky a vast column of smoke and steam; recalling, with a shock of surprise, that, even though the coincidence may have been accidental, Reginald Heber should have so well caught this striking feature of so remote and unknown a ritual: —

"*Smokes* on Gerizim's Mount, Samaria's sacrifice."

Out of the pit were dragged, successively, the six sheep, on their long spits, black from the oven. The

[1] Mishna, *Pesachim*, vi. 7.   [2] Ex. xii. 8, 9.   [3] *Ibid.* 45, 48.

outlines of their heads, their ears, their legs, were still visible, — "his head with his legs, and with the inward parts thereof."[1] They were hoisted aloft and then thrown on large square brown mats, previously prepared for their reception, on which we were carefully prevented from treading, as also from touching even the extremities of the spits. The bodies thus wrapt in the mats were hurried down to the trench where the sacrifice had taken place, and laid out upon them in a line between two files of the Samaritans. Those who had before been dressed in white robes still retained them, with the addition now, of shoes on their feet and staves in their hands, and ropes round their waists, — " Thus shall ye eat it; with your loins girded, your shoes on your feet, your staff in your hand."[2] The recitation of prayers or of the Pentateuch recommenced, and continued, till it suddenly terminated in their all sitting down on their haunches, after the Arab fashion at meals, and beginning to eat. This, too, is a deviation from the practice of only a few years since, when they retained the Mosaic ritual of standing whilst they ate. The actual feast was conducted in rapid silence as of men in hunger, as no doubt most of them were, and so as soon to consume every portion of the blackened masses, which they tore away piecemeal with their fingers, — " Ye shall eat in haste."[3] There was a general merriment, as of a hearty and welcome meal. In ten minutes all was gone but a few remnants. To the Priest and to the women, who, all but two (probably his two wives), remained in the tents, separate morsels were carried round. The rem-

[1] Ex. xii. 9.   [2] *Ibid.* 11.
[3] *Ibid.* 11. The hasty *snatching* which I had heard described, I was unable to recognize.

nants were gathered into the mats, and put on a wooden grate or hurdle over the hole where the water had been originally boiled; the fire was again lit, and a huge bonfire was kindled. By its blaze, and by candles lighted for the purpose, the ground was searched in every direction, as for the consecrated particles of sacramental elements; and these fragments of the flesh and bone were thrown upon the burning mass. "Ye shall let nothing remain until the morning; and that which remaineth until the morning ye shall burn with fire." "There shall not anything of the flesh which thou sacrificest the first day at even remain all night until the morning." "Thou shalt not carry forth aught of the flesh abroad out of the house."[1] The flames blazed up once more, and then gradually sank away. Perhaps in another century the fire on Mount Gerizim will be the only relic left of this most interesting and ancient rite. By the early morning the whole community had descended from the mountain, and occupied their usual habitations in the town. "Thou shalt turn in the morning, and go unto thy tents."[2]

With us it was the morning of Palm Sunday, and it was curious to reflect by what a long gradation of centuries the simple ritual of the English Church — celebrated then, from the necessity of the case, with more than its ordinary simplicity — had grown up out of the wild, pastoral, barbarian, yet still elaborate, commemoration, which we had just witnessed, of the escape of the sons of Israel from the yoke of the Egyptian King.

[1] Ex. xii. 10, 46; Deut. xvi. 4.   [2] Deut. xvi. 7.

I subjoin a few remarks on the situation and antiquities of Shechem, as we saw them on that day to greater advantage than is usually the case; partly from again enjoying the guidance of Dr. Rosen, who has devoted much attention [1] to the neighborhood of Nablûs, partly from the check imposed on the usual fanaticism of the inhabitants by the presence of the Prince of Wales.

As the view of Jerusalem from Mount Olivet reveals all the peculiar features of the southern capital, so does the view from a huge projecting crag of Gerizim — which Dr. Rosen, with great probability, conjectures to have been the position of Jotham as described in the Book of Judges — reveal all the peculiar features of the northern capital Shechem. The view sweeps the whole valley, and shows how completely it is in the very central draught (so to speak) of Palestine. Alone of the cities of the Holy Land, it commands the sight at once of the Trans-Jordanic mountains on the east, and of the broad sea on the west. Opposite, on the north, runs the long ridge of Ebal, evidently the necropolis of the ancient city, which, being itself deep in the valley, required the mountain (and not, as at Jerusalem, the ravine) for its tombs. Behind is Gerizim, sheltering in its northeastern curves the little mosque which, in its various names of *Allon Moreh* (the Oak of Moreh), *Ahron Moreh* (the Ark of Moreh), *Sheykh el Amad* (the Saint of the Pillar), seems to commemorate the tradition of the consecrated oak and treasures of

---

[1] *Zeitschrift Deutsch. Morgenländ. Gesellschaft*, xiv. 634.

Jacob and the pillar of Joshua.[1] Close by in the mountain-side are the vast caverns, overhung with luxuriant creepers, from which Jotham may have issued on the day of his famous parable.[2] Immediately below lies the mass of various verdure, — unparalleled in Palestine, — which gave him the materials for his imagery; the Olives taking the precedence from their size and number; but melting into the richer green of the Fig-tree and the Vine; and all of them towering above the worthless Brier that creeps along the walls.

The actual *shoulder* (Shechem) which may seem to have given its name to the ancient town is a watershed, is exceedingly low, like all those between the Jordan and the Mediterranean, and rises a little to the east of the present town, and thus nearer to the well-known localities of the Consecrated Pillar and of Jacob's Well. But the general situation of the place must have been determined, then as now, by the mighty burst of waters from the flank of Gerizim. Thirty-two springs can be traced in different parts. One of them (*Ain Karoun*) is cherished with an almost religious veneration. Partly from the architecture of the vault erected over it, partly from its non-Arabic name, it seems to have been one of the sacred springs so commonly found in the Eastern Church under the name of *Hagiasma*, itself perhaps, in the heathen times of Neapolis, venerated as the centre of a Pagan Nymphæum. The chief mosques are three.

The Eagle Mosque (*Nasr*) and the Great Mosque

---

[1] See *Sinai and Palestine*, chap. v.
[2] Judg. ix. 7. See *Lectures on the Jewish Church*, p. 386, (Amer. ed.)

(*El Khebir*) have, I believe, been very rarely, if ever, in the memory of man, visited by Europeans. They are both formed out of Christian churches. Both have the form of a Basilica, though the Great Mosque, which was formerly a church of S. John, has a fine Gothic porch, probably built by the Knights of S. John during the Latin occupation of Palestine. Both have columns of Egyptian granite; of which one in the Great Mosque has the completely Egyptian style, both in its capital and in its coloring.

The third mosque is remarkable not for its Christian but for its Samaritan antiquities. It is called "*Hadra*" (" the Green "), or " *Hussn-el-Yakoub* " (" the Wailing Place of Jacob "), from the Mussulman tradition that there Jacob lamented the death of his favorite son, and that the aged mulberry-tree which stands in the court withered at the news of the loss of Joseph, and became green again on his recovery. The mosque has fragments of ancient columns built into its walls, and is said to stand on the site of the ancient synagogue of the Samaritans, erected B. C. 116, when their temple was destroyed by Hyrcanus. A stone is built into the tower of the minaret, inscribed with the Samaritan version of the Ten Commandments, and ending, as if by a combination of the Morning and Evening prayers of the Israelite encampment, — " Arise, O Lord, and turn again." [1]

The existing synagogue stands close by. I leave to Hebrew and Samaritan scholars the vexed question of the relative antiquity of the rolls which are exhibited. A photograph was taken of that which claimed to be the oldest, and which is believed by Dr. Rosen to be

[1] Num. xi. 35, 36. See Sermon XI.

at least as ancient as the destruction of the Samaritan Temple B. C. 116. The dark spots which appear on its surface are said to be from the kisses of the devout Samaritans, imprinted on all the passages where the name or the benediction of Aaron occurs. The hangings in which the cases are wrapt are remarkable as being embroidered with the emblems of the Jewish worship, — amongst which the cherubs appear as birds, and the altar is represented by a grate, much resembling the hurdles over the fire in the Paschal Sacrifice on Mount Gerizim.

GALILEE.

III. GALILEE.

FROM Nablûs we passed by Samaria to Jenin. Here the plain of Esdraelon lay spread out before us. In skirting its southwestern corner on the following day, we crossed the ancient road from Damascus to Egypt, by which of old the Midianite merchants passed when from the neighboring Dothan they carried off their youthful slave;[1] and by which in later times Pharaoh Neco marched and encountered Josiah at Hadad-Rimon, probably a Syrian sanctuary or caravanserai, built by the Damascene caravans.[2] We then traversed the battle-field of Deborah and Barak, and saw how from Taanach the Canaanite[3] host must have watched the army of Barak descending from Tabor which there breaks into view, and how the "waters" of the numerous brooks, which descend from Megiddo, must in the tempest of that memorable day have swelled the stream of the Kishon till it swept away the horses and chariots of the enemy. We encamped under the inland extremity of Carmel, by the green hill of *Tell Kaimon*, probably the ancient *Jokneam;* and thence ascended by the rocky dells and tangled thickets of Carmel to the scene of the sacrifice

[1] Gen. xxxvii. 17, 25.
[2] 2 Kings xxiii. 29. Zech. xii. 11.
[3] See *Lectures on the Jewish Church*, p. 357, (Am. ed.)

of Elijah,[1] where just before sunset was spread out before us the view on which the King and the Prophet had looked on the evening of their long conflict.

The next day we crossed the Kishon, as it forces its way between the flank of Carmel and the projection of the Galilean hills, into the plain of Acre. Over that plain, teeming with game and wild animals of all kinds, we at last reached the groves of palm and orange trees that mark the neighborhood of Acre; and emerged on the cheering and romantic view of the Mediterranean waters, dashing round the curve of the little bay and against the walls of that famous city. From those walls, under the guidance of one of our party who had been present at the time, we explored the traces of the siege of 1840; and, after a midday repast in the ruined gardens of Abdallah Pasha, finally struck across the plain into the mountains of Galilee to the secluded and picturesque village of Shefa Omar.

From this point, the new route, on which I entered in passing through Galilee, afforded many illustrations to my former journey. The forest scenery, which I had known before only from others, I now was able to see for myself. Its chief luxuriance lies between the plain of Acre and the plain of Asochis, or, as it is now called, "the Buttauf." It is a continual succession of parklike glades, abounding in those "birds of the air," of brilliant plumage, which so often figure in the Galilean Parables. It ends abruptly on the western edge of the plain of Buttauf, which on the eastern side is

---

[1] See *Sinai and Palestine*, c. ix. I cannot forbear to express my hope that no mistaken zeal will be encouraged to cover this interesting and sacred site with the church or chapel of any particular sect, as was apprehended a year ago.

bounded by the bare hills of Nazareth. On that western edge, planted on a rocky spur of the hills, is the deserted village, which, according to the oldest local tradition and the most recent critical researches, has been identified with "Cana of Galilee." If, as has been not unreasonably conjectured from the language of S. John's Gospel,[1] Cana was the scene not merely of the occasional visits recorded, but of a lengthened residence of our Lord in Galilee, its site becomes doubly interesting. The name by which the place is now known is still "*Ghana*," or "*Khana*." The affix *El Jelil*, which Dr. Robinson[2] believed to be a still further token of its identity with Cana *of* Cana of Galilee, I never heard in the neighborhood Galilee. nor on the spot. It has every characteristic which the slight indications in the Gospel narrative require. It is about four hours' journey from Nazareth; about an hour's journey from Sepphorieh, the traditional birthplace of the Virgin, the seat of the Roman capital of Galilee, Dio-Cæsarea. The ruins of the modern, and the vestiges of the ancient, village cover the rocky slope of the hill which overhangs the northernmost extremity of the plain. At the time of our visit (in the middle of April) at this part of the plain was a swamp, almost a lake,[3] from the accumulation of recent rain. It is probably from the neighborhood of this swamp that the place derived its name of *Cana*, or the *Reedy;* and the epithet of *Galilee* was added to distinguish it from another *Cana*,[4] one of the streams that flow into the Mediterranean, and so called doubtless for a similar reason, in

---

[1] John ii. 1; iv. 46.   [2] *Biblical Researches*, ii. 346.
[3] From the top of Carmel it had quite the appearance of a lake.
[4] Joshua xvi. 8; xvii. 8.

the tribe of Ephraim. Even on the dry rocky hill a few tall reeds were growing amidst a quantity of fennel, to vindicate the justice of the appellation. The ground is perforated with several deep cavities. They might have been tombs; but were more probably cisterns. Close under the village is a deep well, whence, if the identification be correct, must have been the water " which filled the water-pots up to the brim." [1] Over one of the cavities a fig-tree — the only tree, if I rightly remember, on the spot — spread its wide green leaves, and recalled the shade of that fig-tree [2] under which was seen, by the token that called him to Christ, the one native of the village whose name has come down to us, " Nathanael of Cana of Galilee." [3] This is all that can be said to identify the spot. Yet, if it be the place, the interest is enhanced by finding that it stands at the entrance of one of the few wooded glens in Palestine which can really claim to be called beautiful; and of which the romantic scenery, at least to our modern notions, harmoniously blends with the gay yet primitive festivity of that wedding-day which has cast its brightness over all the marriages of Christendom.

The glen leads, by a steep ascent of half an hour's ride, into the presence of a locality of strangely different associations. A huge wooded hill, parted from the neighboring mountains by a deep, dry watercourse, and called by the neighboring Arabs " *Shafat,*" or " *Jafat,*" is, beyond all question, the *Jotapata,*[4] of

[1] John ii. 7.
[2] John i. 50.
[3] John xxi. 2.
[4] Joseph. *B. J.* iii. 7. This, as well as the situation of Cana, is very well given in Dr. Schultz's map of Galilee. By the assistance of this map, when once in the Plain of Buttauf, we found these localities without a guide.

Josephus. There the Galilean Jews intrenched themselves in a fortress, of which the ruins still remain scattered over the hill; and there Josephus, by his final surrender of himself to the Roman army, saved the life which his writings have rendered so far more valuable than he or Vespasian could at that time possibly have anticipated. The spot, in connection with those writings, is remarkable, as an instance of their general exactness, combined with special inaccuracies. On the one hand, the precipices are here, as in his account of Jerusalem, prodigiously exaggerated. On the other hand, the one singular peculiarity of the place is caught and described. The hill is, as he says, enclosed in other hills; and, though so large and lofty in itself, is invisible till you are close upon it.

Good Friday was spent at Nazareth. The furious storm which on that day raged through the whole of Syria, rendered it impossible to do more than Nazareth. visit the well-known sanctuaries in the village.[1] In passing from one to the other, it was curious to observe the different Eastern applications — so different from our own — of the names of the great theological divisions of Christendom. "What is this Church?" I asked from my Arab guide. "The Church of Rome," he replied, meaning "the Church of New Rome — of Constantinople — of the Roman Empire — of Greece." "And this?" "The Catholic Church;" meaning the Church of the Greeks who have become united to the Roman Catholic Church, commonly called "United Greeks" or "Greek Catholics." "And this?" "The Latin;" meaning the Roman Catholic Church, to which he himself belonged. We encamped by the

[1] See *Sinai and Palestine*, c. x. xiv.

Spring of the Annunciation. Its source is within the small Greek Church; and it thence flows out into the neighboring olive-grove to supply the town. Under the guidance of Mr. Zeller, the Protestant Missionary, stationed at Nazareth, we explored the remains of the ancient cisterns on the hillside, which seem to indicate both the antiquity of the situation, and also the fact that the old town was on a somewhat higher elevation than the modern.

On the following day we ascended Mount Tabor. Mount Tabor is the easternmost and southernmost extremity of the forestlike park which, overlapping the plain of Asochis and the hills of Nazareth, here runs out as if for one expiring effort into the green woods which clothe the whole of the lower part of this famous mountain. Its connection with Barak, its disconnection from the scene of the Transfiguration,[1] I have indicated elsewhere. But there are a few particulars attached to its modern history which demand a notice here. The fortress of which the ruins crown the summit had evidently four gateways, like those by which the great Roman camps of our own country were entered. By one of these gateways, Mr. Zeller called my attention to an Arabic inscription, which he had discovered on the spot, the only one on the mountain. It lies on a broken fragment, and runs as follows: — "In the name of God, the Compassionate, the Merciful, those that spend their property for the glory of God, and do not grudge what they have spent, will be rewarded. Their reward is from their God, and they have nothing to fear, nor will they suffer. Our Lord, the mighty Sultan, the victorious, the sword of the

[1] See *Sinai and Palestine*, c. ix.

world and of the faith, the Sultan of Islam, the King
Abubeker, the son of Khalil, the Prince of the Faithful, ordered,[1] the building of this blessed fortress on his
return from the East. The commencement of the
work was on the first day of the week, the fifth day of
the month Zilhijy, in the year 607. During the administration of the Emir Ahmehdin-Lemin, the son of
Abdallah, the great King."

The contentions of the Holy Places have penetrated even to the broad summit of this lonely mountain.
It is parcelled out in enclosures, belonging respectively
to the Greek and Latins; one portion was ploughed
by the Mussulmans to prevent its occupation by the
Christians; but it has been regained by one or other
of the rival churches. On the eastern extremity is
rising a Greek church, which owes its origin to the following story, curious as illustrating many legends of
earlier times. A Wallachian monk, of the name of
Erinna, is said to have received an intimation in his
sleep that he was to build a church on a mountain
shown to him in a dream.[2] He wandered through
many countries, and found his mountain at last in
Tabor. There he lived on a tree which still remains,
and collected money from pilgrims, which at his death,
a few years ago, amounted to a sufficient sum to raise
the Church. He professed to be more than a hundred
years of age, and he was remarkable for his long beard,
and for a tame panther, which, like the ancient hermits, he was supposed to have as his constant companion.

[1] By "building" is probably meant "restoration." The date (in our era) is A. D. 1210. The Sultan spoken of is the brother of Saladin, generally called *Saphadin*.

[2] A similar story is told of the founder of S. John's College, Oxford.

On the way between Tabor and Tiberias, we were received by Aghyle Aga, a well-known Bedouin or half-Bedouin chief in the neighborhood, who, after a life of adventures, somewhat similar to those of David at the court of Achish, had acquired a certain reputation by the protection which he had extended to the Christians of Nazareth and the neighborhood during the disturbances of 1860. The reception was interesting as bringing before us several of the well-known traits of Arabian life depicted in the Bible. The long tent of black goat's hair was entirely open to the leeward side; carpets and rugs were spread on the ground, and a low divan was slightly raised on cushions. The pegs of the tent were rough stakes or pieces of wood. The "hammer" was a large wooden mallet. The wife's tent was the same as the other, only that no one enters it besides herself and the chief, and hence all the valuables are kept there. The meal, for the inadequacy of which Aghyle Aga six times over repeated the most urgent apologies, consisted of three courses. The first was in a large pewter dish filled with small tender pieces of mutton, taken with the fingers. The second was in a pewter barrel, filled with sour milk (*Lebban*), frothed like cream, drunk with a cup, and a smaller pewter bowl, filled with sweet milk (*Haleb*), to be drunk by raising it to the mouth. In both were dipped the large flexible rags of Arab cake or bread, thrown in profusion on the carpets. The third stage consisted of a larger bowl, filled with rice, which the two chiefs, who up to this time had stood by watching our meal, now, when requested to do so, sat down and devoured, rolling up balls of rice in the hollow of their hands, and tossing

Bedouin tents.

the whole handful down their mouths with extraordinary rapidity.

It is almost needless to point out in this the familiar reminiscences of the tent of Abraham and the tent of Jael, those two Biblical pictures of Patriarchal life. There were the entreaties to stay, and partake of the hospitality. "My lord, if now I have found favor in thy sight, pass not away, I pray thee, from thy servant."[1] "Turn in, my lord, turn in to me."[2] There is the meat from the flocks or herds "tender and good,"[3] "hastily dressed, and the morsel of bread to comfort the heart;" "fine meal kneaded, and made into cakes on the hearth."[4] There is the "cream"[5] in "the lordly dish,"[6] as well as the sweet "milk instead of water." There[7] is the host "standing by" whilst the guests did eat."[8] There is the wife's tent close at hand, but free from the intrusion of strangers.[9] There is the divan on which the sleeper might recline, raised above the level ground;[10] and the rugs[11] or carpets to cover him.[12] There is the strong peg or stake of the tent, and the huge wooden mallet to drive it into the ground, or into the sleeper's temples.[13]

On the evening of that day we reached the Lake of Gennesareth. It had been arranged that on the shores of its sacred waters we should pass our Easter Sunday. Far away from the contentions which so lamentably disfigure the relations of the various relig-

[1] Gen. xviii. 3.
[2] Judges iv. 18.
[3] Gen. xviii. 7.
[4] Gen. xviii. 5, 6, 7.
[5] Translated "butter."
[6] Gen. xviii. 8; Judges v. 25.
[7] Gen. xviii. 8; Judges iv. 19, 25.
[8] Gen. xviii. 8.
[9] Gen. xviii. 9; Judges iv. 18, 20.
[10] Judges v. 2.
[11] Translated "mantle."
[12] Judges iv. 18.
[13] Judg. iv. 21; v. 26.

ious communities of Modern Jerusalem, — that Easter Day will be long remembered by every member of the party.

The furious storm of Good Friday, which, we were told, had made the Sea of Tiberias one sheet of snow-white foam, gradually cleared away on Easter Eve. Suddenly, as we rode across the desolate undulations of the plain of Hattîn, we came to the edge of the hills which overhang the lake. When I first saw this view nine years before, I felt, and strove to express [1] that it was a moment, if any, when recollections of the past are too powerful for any criticism of the actual prospect, to determine whether it be tame and poor, as some travellers have said, or eminently beautiful, as others. That hesitation on this second sight of it was entirely removed. No one who stood on those heights on that evening could doubt the surpassing beauty of the scene which lay before him, even had it been devoid of any sacred interest. In one instant, as if through a rent, opening in the earth beneath our feet, flashed the whole expanse of the lake, as it lay in its deep basin a thousand feet below us. The masses of stormy cloud which were still flying to and fro, left clear in the northern sky the white crown of Hermon; and the falling sun threw its soft light over the deep descent, as we wound down the tortuous pathway, round the ruined walls and battlements of Tiberias to our encampment on the silent shore, — a silence broken only by the gentle ripple of the waves on the rough pebbly beach.

And hardly less beautiful was the dawn of the Easter morning, when the sun behind a black bank of

---

[1] *Sinai and Palestine*, c. x. p. 370.

cloud rose over the wall of the mountains on the farther side, themselves still dark in shadow, and poured down its first rays upon the calm waters of the lake, and the gray tops of the western hills were tinged with golden light. . . .

In a long walk in the quiet afternoon of that Easter Day above the shores of the lake almost to its southern end, I was enabled to see more clearly than before the exact scene of the exit of the Jordan. It creeps silently through a flat grassy plain, and winds peacefully through the level. The rapid descent which it makes farther to the south is not here visible. The distant situation of the opening of the valley on this plain through the eastern hills is worth noticing, as showing how completely removed from the shores of the lake is Um-keis (the ancient Gadara), which lies at the head of this valley, and therefore how entirely unsuitable to the incident of the demoniacs[1] in the Gospel narrative, with which it has sometimes in later times been connected.

On the following day we rode along the whole of the western shore northwards.

The general features of the plain of Gennesareth are even more marked than I had before represented them. It is stamped as it were with a peculiar character by the deep rocky glen of the Valley of Doves descending into it from the southwest. The situation of the ancient fortress of Arbela, at the head of this precipitous pass, makes it probable that this rather

[1] I may here take the opportunity of mentioning that a party of Englishmen, who, in 1861, explored the Wady Fik on the Eastern shore (which I had given as the probable scene of the transaction, *Sinai and Palestine*, c. x.), have stated to me considerable difficulties in the way of this identification.

than any town in the level plain of Esdraelon, is the fortress of Betharbel, in which, on the Assyrian invasion, "the mother was dashed to pieces" (thrown down the cliffs as it would seem), "upon her children."[1] The flights of wild hawks, doves, and jays, of brilliant plumage, over the rich plain more forcibly than ever illustrated "the birds of the air" in the Parables spoken by the lake-side; whilst the intermixture of corn-fields, thorn-trees, rocks, and pathways, as represented in the great Parable of the Sower, which I noticed before[2] in a single spot, seems to be characteristic of the whole locality.

The disputed sites of the cities of Gennesareth *Gennesareth.* must still remain disputed. At Khan Minyeh (or Ain-et-Tin,) the traces of artificial work on the rock which overhangs the spring — cuttings as if for streets or roads — add some slight confirmation to the theory that this was the situation of Capernaum.[3] The smooth white beach near Tabigah suggests it as the probable scene of the interview with the Seven Disciples.[4] The solid structures, of which the ruins remain at Tell Hûm, indicate a place of importance; but its distance from the plain, the absence of any spring, and the slightness of the elevation on which they stand, deprive it of any special appropriateness for Capernaum.

From Tell Hûm we rode to the northern extremity of the lake. Here through a level plain, almost a morass, entangled with thickets of oleander, which cluster round its tributary brooks, the Jordan passes into the lake under a group of five isolated palms. It

---

[1] Hosea x. 14.
[2] *Sinai and Palestine*, c. xiii.
[3] *Ibid.* c. x.
[4] John xxi. 3.

is already a turbid stream, carrying its brown color far into the clear lake. But the swift and active descent of its upper course is concealed within the walls of the narrow gorge from which it issues into the plain. The scene well suits the incident described by Josephus,[1] when his horse plunging in the morass threw him off. On the gentle hill which rises immediately at the back of the plain may be traced with sufficient accuracy the situation of the northern Bethsaida, and the scene of the incidents connected with it in the Gospel history. On the first slope of the rising ground are the vestiges of the village (Tell), supposed to mark the site of the old town. On the second stage of the hill, immediately above, is a broad green platform, where on the "much grass"[2] the multitude may have been invited to rest. On the third stage, at the summit of the eminence, is a bare ridge, "the desert place," the mountain to which our Lord may have retired "by Himself alone,"[3] overlooking from end to end the whole lake, with the storm sweeping up it from the south, and His disciples vainly toiling through the waves as the shades of evening closed upon them.[4]

It was two hours after sunset that, at the close of a long day's ride, we mounted the steep ascent by which Safed is approached, and it was a gladdening sound to hear the shout of welcome, almost resembling a British cheer, with which the advanced post of the Jews of Safed greeted in the darkness the approach of the English Prince. Accompanied, preceded, followed by these Jewish colonists, some singing, some playing on tambours, some on foot, some on

Safed.

[1] In his "Life," § 72.
[2] Mark vi. 39 : John iv. 10.
[3] Mark vi. 31, 35, 40; John vi. 15.
[4] Mark vi. 48 ; John vi. 16, 17, 18, 23.

horseback, with their infants in their arms, we reached the encampment under the castle of Safed. It is perched on an elevation so conspicuous as to give rise to the notion that it may have been "the city set on a hill."[1] From the summit of the castle, still rent in many parts from the effects of the great earthquake of 1837, the view commands points in some respects peculiar to itself. To the west and north the mountains of Galilee intercept any further prospect. But on the east, the eye actually looks down upon the flat tops of the Trans-Jordanic hills, — those level, or at least gently undulating plains, which gave that region the name of "Misor," or "the Downs." A conspicuous curving mountain ("Kulcib," "the little heart") marks distinctly the centre of Bashan. The sea of Galilee is unfolded in the most precise and characteristic form, even to the peculiar shape of the plain of Gennesareth, the long precipitous defile of the Valley of Doves, and the broad table plain of Hattin above, crowned with the Mount of Beatitudes. On the slope of the hill to the south, immediately facing Safed, is visible a long low white building which marks the site of Meiron, the burial-place of Hillel and Shammai, the centre of attraction to all the Jewish pilgrims of Northern Palestine.

To be near these tombs, and to be within sight of the sacred lake of Tiberias, seems to have been the object of the colony of European Jews (for such they are), which has congregated on the heights of Safed, and rendered it, in spite of its absolute obscurity or non-existence in earlier times, the fourth of the Holy Places in Palestine in the eyes of modern Judaism.

[1] *Sinai and Palestine,* c. x.

Safed is the modern sanctuary of the territory now occupied by the tribe of Naphtali. A Kedesh-day's journey northwards over bare hills and Naphtali. deep descending valleys, brought us to the site of the true ancient sanctuary of the same great tribe, — Kedesh-Naphtali, the "Holy Place," the "City of Refuge" of the tribe of Naphtali, the residence of Barak, and the scene of the murder of Sisera, — the burial-place, as the Jewish pilgrims of the Middle Ages supposed, of Deborah, Barak, and Jael. Two green plains succeed each other. The first, to the south, is marked by a grove of terebinths. Here, if at all in the neighborhood, was probably "the terebinth of the unloading of tents,"[1] under which Heber the Kenite had pitched his encampment, and to which Sisera fled for refuge. The second to the north, is immediately under a rising ground occupied by the modern village, still bearing the name of *Kedes*. No town in western Palestine, with the exception of Jerusalem, Hebron, and Shechem, has such evident vestiges of antiquity and sacredness, as this remote northern sanctuary. The summit of the hill is strewed with remnants of ancient oil-presses, finely worked capitals,[2] fragments of ancient walls. Tombs of every kind are found in the platform in front, and the valley behind the vil-

---

[1] See *Lectures on the Jewish Church*, p. 361, (Am. ed.)

[2] In the village the head of a female statue was offered to us. It is apparently of a late Phœnician style.

I have dwelt at greater length on Kedesh-Naphtali because, though described with his usual care by Dr. Robinson (*Later Researches*, 367–369), there are in his account a few trifling inaccuracies:—1. He speaks of only one double sarcophagus. There are two. — 2. He omits to mention the eagle sculptured on the portal of the westernmost edifice, which is against his hypothesis of its being a Jewish synagogue. — 3. He did not visit the other tombs, or the remains in the village.

lage; tombs hewn out of the rock,—stone coffins thrust into the side of the hill,—richly ornamented sarcophaguses, raised on pedestals, double, as if for man and wife. Not far from these last are the remains of a solid massive building, believed by Dr. Robinson to have been a synagogue, but, from the eagle carved on its portal, as at Baalbec, more probably a heathen temple. Of all these remains there is absolutely no history. We can but conjecture that they are the continuation, probably through different religions, of the original sanctity attached to the place on the first conquest of Joshua; if, indeed, that was not itself engrafted on some earlier Canaanite worship, bound up with the flowing springs and the green fields that must always have given the spot a name and a significance. There,—within sight of the city of Jabin, his king, on the one hand (for wherever Hazor be, it cannot be far distant), and the city of Barak, his conqueror,—Sisera perished by the hand of Jael.

The hills, which between Safed and Kedesh-Naphtali had been mostly bare, shortly afterwards, farther north, were tufted with trees and thickets. And on each side the prospect opens so as to include the best views of this part of the country. On the west, the hills of Naphtali extend to the sea. In the midst of them on a crested height stands the castle of Tibnîn, seat of the Metâwileh chiefs, whose tribes inhabit the whole of this region. On the east, lies the plain of the Upper Jordan; the whole lake of Hûleh (or Merom) spread out in its wide basin, and on the north the white cone of Lebanon, and the white wall of Hermon. From the castle of Tibnîn came Tamer

Bey, the Metâwileh chief,[1] with his magnificent hawks. Far over the hills the party was scattered with a wide dispersion, such as exactly recalled the incidents so well described by Sir Walter Scott in the hawking scene of the "Betrothed." In different groups we descended through the woods, by the fine castle of Hunin, down into the vale of the Jordan, crossed with difficulty its many tributaries, and finally assembled for our last mid-day meal in Palestine under the venerable oak of Dan, which overhangs the Lower source of the Jordan.

That evening we reached the upper source of the river at Banias,[2] and climbed to the little chapel of S. George, above the cliff and the cave, from which the sacred river issues. Our first day in the Holy Land had led us through the ancient cathedral of the patron saint whom the English Crusaders brought back with them from Palestine; our last, on S. George's day (April 23), found us by this small shrine, where he is revered as a Mussulman saint.

And now, having followed the scenes of the Gospel history through "Judea, Samaria, and Galilee," we parted from them at the last spot to which the journeys of our Lord can be traced, — "the coasts of Cæsarea Philippi."[3]

[1] The Metâwileh tribes, who inhabit these hills, are a colony of "Shiahs," the Persian disciples of Ali. M. Renan told me that he had seen pictures of the Shah of Persia in their cottages.
I mention this, because notices appeared in some foreign journals that the Prince of Wales had been received with acclamations by the Druze chiefs. The Druze chiefs we never saw. The mistake probably arose from this one day's meeting with the leaders of the Metâwileh tribes from Tibnin.

[2] *Sinai and Palestine*, c. XI.   [3] Matt. xvi. 13.

HERMON AND LEBANON.

IV. HERMON AND LEBANON.

THE remaining period of our stay in Syria was devoted to those two great parallel mountain ranges from which the whole physical structure of Syria takes its rise.[1]

On leaving the Holy Land, the interest of the country changes its character. It belongs for the most part to secular geography and history. But this secondary interest is of so peculiar a kind and attaches itself so closely to the Land, of which these regions form the outposts, that a few words may be added to fill up the very imperfect account given of these parts in my former work.

We were enabled to explore the two singular valleys which intersect the lower regions of these great mountain chains. The first is the Wady-et-teim. Wady-et-Teim. This is the valley which divides from each other the southern portions of the Lebanon and Anti-Lebanon, as the Beka'a or Cœle Syria divides their northern portions. It is formed by the Hasbany River, — the river of Hasbeya, — which is, in strict geography though not in history, the highest branch and source of the Jordan. It has a sacredness of its own, though neither Biblical nor classical, as the chief seat of the Druzes, who settling there in the eleventh century,

[1] See *Sinai and Palestine*, c. xii.

under their founder Derazy, have since spread through the surrounding hills and valleys in every direction.

The range which forms the western boundary of the Wady-et-Teim is, in fact, the south-eastern spur of Lebanon; and from the highest ridge of this is obtained one of the best geographical views (if I may so express myself) that I ever saw. The double lines of Lebanon and Anti-Lebanon are full in sight; and the Jordan is visible in all its upper stages, through the whole length of the valley of its northern tributary the Hasbany; through the whole valley of the lake of Merom, down through the opening gap, to the waters still distinct, and seen for the last time, of the lake of Gennesareth. The Litâny[1] (or Leontes) flows beneath. It parts asunder the two portions of Lebanon, which else would naturally be one; and which still cling so closely to each other that the dividing river is almost lost in their narrow embrace. This is the peculiarity which has of late years given such a stimulus to the curiosity of travellers concerning it. From the moment that it leaves the broad plain of Cœle Syria, in which it rises, it plunges into a long ravine, so deep and so precipitous that its course can with difficulty be traced from the overhanging brow of the rocky eminences which close it on either side. And it so completely cuts off communication from either side to the other that, but for a singular freak of nature, no intercourse could take place across its banks for a course of nearly thirty miles. This fortunate freak is the natural bridge (the Kûweh), which consists of a solid mass of earth or rock that has fallen over its course, and in that one single spot, at the foot of the rocks, allows of

---

[1] See *Sinai and Palestine*, c. xii.

a transit from east to west of the stream.¹ So it rushes through this dark and winding depth till, at the first wider opening which it meets, it suddenly turns westward under the huge precipice of the castle of Esh-Shŭkîf or Belfort; a castle, as its name implies, built by the Crusaders, but raised on the foundations or out of the remains of some older fortress, intended to guard the gorge, which once more closes in and conveys this most furious, but most secluded, of rivers into the Mediterranean Sea not far from Tyre.

From this wild valley and mysterious river, the passage over Mount Hermon, or Anti-Lebanon, again brought us within the range of an antique sanctity, of which the traces remain everywhere, but of which the precise origin is veiled in obscurity.

I have elsewhere² shown that Mount Hermon is probably the true scene of the Transfiguration, the " high mountain "³ above Cæsarea Philippi ; and, if so, the only one of all the eminences mentioned in the New Testament, which is called " the Holy Mountain."⁴ In the Old Testament, besides the names of Hermon, Senir, and Sion, it seems also to have borne that of Baal-Hermon, " the sanctuary ⁵ of Hermon." Of this sacredness the proofs are manifold. It is, as

---

¹ The description of this bridge and of the Litâny generally, is admirably given by Dr. Robinson (*Lat. Res.* 422-424), though with a touch of exaggeration very unusual in his sober pages. I cannot quote this work without again bearing my humble testimony (with such slight exceptions as I have here and elsewhere ventured to notice) to his rare merits as an accurate, observant, and powerful describer of physical and historical geography.
² *Sinai and Palestine*, c. xi.   ³ Matt. xvii. 1.
⁴ 2 Peter i. 18.
⁵ Judges iii. 3. "Mount Baal Hermon." See Mr. Grove on this word in the Dictionary of the Bible.

Dr. Robinson truly remarks, "girded with ancient temples.[1] They are found in all situations; crowning hills and mountain tops, or secluded in valleys and deep gorges. The founders and worshippers have disappeared for unknown ages;[2] whether they were Phœnicians or Græco-Syrians we cannot tell; they have left behind no trace but these their works, and no record how or why these works were erected." That on its summit, of which some ruins are still to be traced,[3] was noticed by Jerome. To this, on its heights or in its close neighborhood, may be added no less than eighteen. Seven are to be seen on its more southern uplands, Rūkleh, Kul'at Bostra, Hibbâryieh, Neby Sūfa, Deir-el-Ashayr, Burkush. That of Neby Sūfa "stands facing the east,[4] directly over against Hermon, in his most imposing aspect." That of Hibbâryieh " fronts directly on the great chasm of Wady Shiba, looking up the mighty gorge, as if to catch the first beams of the morning sun rising over Hermon."[5] That of Rūkleh, which is further east, "fronts westward" also "towards the Mount of Hermon," and is distinguished by a finely-carved human countenance, as if intended for Baal or Astarte.[6] That of Deir-el-Ashayr[7] fronts eastward, and is remarkable as consisting of a double edifice, one below the other;[8] as on a larger scale at Baalbec.

Eleven more can be traced in the passes of the Anti-Lebanon westward of Damascus. One, indeed

[1] Rob. *Lat. Res.* 432.
[2] *Ibid.* iii. 418.
[3] Porter in Rob. *Lat. Res.* 432.
[4] Rob. *Lat. Res.* iii. 426.
[5] *Ibid.* 417.
[6] *Ibid.* 436.
[7] *Ibid.* 437.
[8] Of this there is a representation in Mr. Bedford's Photographs; probably the only one ever taken of the ruins.

two, stand over the source of Ain Fijeh, as if to consecrate that most abundant of all the Syrian springs, the supposed source of the Barada. Large traces of another, also in connection with the river, are to be seen at Kefr Zeit.[1] Another, of which the many columnar fragments give its name to the village where they are found, " Kefr-el-Awamîd," "the village of the columns," is near Abila, and must have faced towards the sacred hill, now crowned by the alleged tomb of Abel; the tomb itself, as it would seem, planted on a more ancient sanctuary. Two or three cluster on the slopes of the hill below Bludân. By one of these stands a clump of aged ilexes, perhaps, with the exception of that of Hazuri, near Banias, the best likeness in Syria of the ancient groves of Astarte. On a rude altar among the trees, by an immemorial usage which has given to the spot the name of Um-es-Shu-kakîf,[2] " the mother of fragments," the neighboring villagers are in the habit of breaking earthen jars. The hill of Nebi Yunas (the Prophet Jonah), above Bludân, is, in like manner, full of similar remains. At its foot, in the plain of Suraya, are two evidently consecrated to the spring which gushes out from its rocks (*Ain Fowar*). Half way up is a third; on its summit are two, one of more antique appearance than the other; both commanding a magnificent view of Hermon and the surrounding valleys.[3]

Two or three other temples exist not far off: Medjil, further south, and Ain Ata, farther north, in the plain

[1] Robinson, *Lat. Res.* 478.
[2] Porter's *Five Years in Damascus*, i. 281.
[3] To this array of heathen sanctuaries must be added the legends of later Jewish or Mussulman tradition which are given in *Sinai and Palestine*, c. xii.

of the Beka'a, or Cœle Syria. But Baalbec stands supreme, and may well close the series which has been given of the sanctuaries of Anti-Lebanon. Its identification with any Biblical site must remain extremely uncertain. It may possibly be Baalath, the frontier city of Solomon, or Baal-Hamon, the pleasure garden of the Canticles, or Baal-Hermon, the "sanctuary of Baal in Hermon," or Baal Gad[1] ("the gathering of Baal,") "under Hermon." Against each of these suppositions there are objections, which must prevent us from coming to any positive conclusion on the subject. Of the general importance of Baalbec in ancient times, however, there can be no question.

The size and beauty of the buildings render them at once a physical landmark and a historical monument which no notice of Syria ought to omit. "In vastness of plan combined with elaborateness and delicacy of execution, they seemed to surpass all others in Western Asia, in Africa, and in Europe." The ranges of columns[2] which give to the edifices their peculiar grace belong to the same age of later Roman magnificence which has left so many proud memorials of itself throughout the East. But there are touches of an earlier antiquity which give it a true connection with the history of Palestine and Egypt.

Its situation was probably fixed by the necessity of a sanctuary to greet the travellers and merchants on the great caravan route between Damascus and Tyre,

---

[1] *Baalath* (1 Kings ix. 28), *Baal-Hamon*, Cant. viii. 11, *Baal-hermon*, 1 Chron. v. 23; Judges iii. 3. *Baal Gad*, Joshua xi. 16. Several of these names may in fact be synonymous for the same place. Baalath is advocated by Mr. Hogg (*The Names of Baalbec*, p. 2–4.) Baal Gad by Ritter (ii. 230).

[2] Robinson's *Lat. Res.* 517.

as Petra between Damascus and the Gulf of Elath. Its name, even if we cannot connect it with any Biblical spot, evidently points to its connection with Baal, — " the assembly or gathering of Baal," [1] — as its Greek name " Heliopolis " shows the identification of Baal with the Sun. Baal was in Greek mythology, identified, as the supreme God, with Jupiter; as the Sun-god with Apollo; and hence in the descriptions of different temples included in the vast sanctuary has arisen, both in ancient and modern times, a confusion between the two which it is now almost impossible to rectify.[2] Like the temples of Baal [3] at Samaria and at Gades,[4] it included the inferior deities as well as the chief Sun-god himself. " To the Gods of Heliopolis" is the inscription which still testifies to the plurality of divinities worshipped there.

The influence of Egypt is indicated not only by the legend of the sacred image [5] brought from the Egyptian city of the sun, — " On " " Heliopolis," but by some striking peculiarities of Egyptian architecture : as for example, the Egyptian symbol of a winged globe is in one of the recesses of the great court; an Egyptian capital crowns one of the columns of the lesser Temple; and the crested eagle with its outspread wings in the portal occupies the same relative position, and apparently represents the same idea, as the blue wings over the Egyptian doorways. " Under the shadow of

---

[1] " Bekka," is the same word as " Mecca," the *m* and *b* being interchanged as in the name *Baalbec* itself, sometimes *Mualbec*. *Bec* is to press, as in a crowd; *Mek*, to suck out as a young camel the milk from the udder. I derive this information from Dr. Vandyck, of Beirût.
[2] See Mr. Hogg on the Names of Baalbec, p. 47.
[3] 2 Kings x. 26, 27.
[4] Liv. xxi. 22.
[5] Macrobius, Saturn. i. 23 (Robinson's *Lat. Res.* 518.)

thy wings shall be my refuge," is the more general expression in which the figure appears in the Biblical imagery. "The *son of* righteousness shall rise with healing in *his wings*,"[1] is the figure which is more directly illustrated by the eagle of Baalbec.

Finally, the huge substructions of the outer enclosure probably point to the earliest foundation of the building, Phœnician, Jewish, or Syrian. The three vast stones, which for a long period gave to the whole building the name of the "Threestone" (*Trilithon*), exceed in size even those of Hebron or Jerusalem, and with the still vaster stone[2] on which they rest, and which has nearly escaped observation from its being also the corner-stone of the wall, present the most gigantic masses of hewn stone that are to be found in the world. In the adjacent quarry are to be seen the stones still standing cut out of the rock, like tall trees waiting to be felled; one already lies prostrate with the lines drawn across its two ends, as if for the cutting off of the unfinished part.

Within the precincts of the temple of Baalbec, the worship of Baal lingered to the latest days of Paganism,[3] with a union of licentiousness and ferocity which renders the spot a memorial of the ancient Canaanite religion, on its darker side, as its magnificence and beauty recall the brighter and nobler side of the faith of the whole ancient world.

I have given this brief summary of the sanctuaries of the Anti-Lebanon, because some of them were new to me, and because attention has hardly been suffi-

---

[1] Malachi iv. 2.
[2] It is of a darker color and is hewn away at the top. It is sixty-eight feet long; the others are sixty-four.
[3] Robinson's *Lat. Res.* 522, 523.

ciently called to the number of temples which attest its ancient sanctity.

In point of time, in the Prince's tour, Baalbec intervened between the two chief cities of the Anti-Lebanon and Lebanon, Damascus and Beirût. It was after leaving Hasbeya and Rasheya, both memorable as being the first scenes of the massacres of 1860, — that we approached Damascus by that splen- Damascus. did view [1] which I need not here again describe, but which still appeared to me to stand amongst the foremost in the world. There are other views more beautiful or more instructive. There can hardly be another at once so beautiful and so instructive. " This is indeed worth all the toil and danger which it has cost me to come here," was the expression used but a few days later on the same spot by the distinguished writer [2] whose premature death at Damascus, almost immediately afterwards, gave a mournful significance to words which every traveller will feel to be true.

Our descent to the city was accompanied by the crowd and tumult which always greeted the Prince's arrival. But it is worth noticing, as a proof of the deeply seated irritation of the Mussulman population of Damascus against the Powers of Christendom, that, here alone of all the Eastern cities through which he passed, was there any indication of a wish to withhold the respect due to his rank and position. Along the streets and bazaars many a Mussulman remained sullen and immovable on his seat, instead of rising to salute the long cavalcade as it approached. A message from

[1] *Sinai and Palestine,* c. xii.
[2] Henry Thomas Buckle died at Damascus, May 29, 1862.

the Pasha afterwards corrected this unusual sign of aversion to the appearance of a Christian Prince. But the natural feeling of the populace was not to be mistaken.

It was in the interval between my two visits that the terrible tragedy had taken place, which will render the summer of 1860 forever dark in the annals of Damascus.

The story of these events, which we heard on the spot from eye-witnesses, has been told, and will doubtless often be told again in a fuller shape than can be given here. But the view of the Christian quarter, as we saw it, will gradually disappear, and with it the actual monument (so to speak) of the great catastrophe. From well-built streets we passed into a vast scene of ruin, extending over probably a fourth part of the city. A few buildings were rising again, but most of the houses remained nearly in the condition in which they were discovered after having been fired and plundered. In those of the wealthy merchants the traces of gilding and painting still remained on the broken walls. The great church of the Greek Patriarcharte of Syria, which had for many generations been transferred to Damascus from Antioch, and has been since these events transferred from Damascus to Beirût, is shattered to pieces. Mosaics, marble columns, cloisters, have all disappeared. One vast mosaic alone of the Virgin is left, riddled with shot; and the marble pavement of the altar can still be traced, to which the Christians fled for refuge, and were there slaughtered by hundreds, like the Jews in the last siege of Jerusalem. Abd-el-Kader, the soldier and theologian united in one, whose heroic resistance to the fanaticism of his co-religionists furnishes so rare an example of this virtue, rare both to Mussulmans and Christians, received with graceful modesty the compliments which the Prince paid to him for his conduct on this occasion. "It was no more than my duty. My religion would not allow me to do otherwise than I did." So deep an impression had been made upon his mind by the transaction, that, when asked some questions respecting the books of the Old Testament, the only remark which he made in answer was that he believed the massacres of Damascus to have been foretold by the Prophet Isaiah — alluding, no doubt, to the words "Damascus shall be a ruinous heap,"[1] — as true of the city after this devastation by its own inhabitants, as after any of its many sieges by foreign invaders.

Of the antiquities and traditional localities of Damascus, I saw much more than on my former visit, chiefly through the kindness and intelligence of the excellent Presbyterian missionary, Mr. Robson.

The great Mosque, once the Church of S. John, formerly a heathen temple, till the last two years had been closed against Christians. The main cause of this exclusion was the fear lest they should gain access to a sacred room, where (as in the Mosque of Omar at Jerusalem) every prayer is presumed to be granted. It is a small chamber, begrimed with dust, and covered with the names of Mussulman pilgrims, in what is called the Minaret of Isa (Jesus), so called from the belief that on that minaret, and into that chamber, He will descend to judge the world.

The "Place" or Mosque of Abraham, at Birzeh, about four miles from Damascus, to which attention

[1] Isaiah xvii. 1.

had been called since my first visit, I now saw, and have elsewhere described at length.[1] In itself it has but little interest. But its situation is remarkable, in the corner of the vast plain, just where the bare hills, intersected by a deep ravine, descend on the mass of verdure which reaches up to the very foot of the rocks. Its connection with Abraham is the oldest local tradition which can be ascertained in or around Damascus.

The "Straight Street,"[2] the "Via Recta" of the Roman city, is apparent to any careful observer. The eastern entrance of the main thoroughfare of the modern town is a triple gateway of Roman architecture. It is evident that each of its three arches opened upon a street — the central arch on the broad highway — the two lesser ones on the side streets, parted from the main street by colonnades, of which a few fragments still remain. For about a hundred yards, the straight direction of this thoroughfare is still discernible. It is then choked up by houses and bazaars; but enough remains to prove that it once ran, like all the main streets in the rectangular cities of the Syro-Grecian or Syro-Roman times, right through Damascus. The traditional "house of Judas," where St. Paul lodged, is sufficiently within the track to render the tradition possible.

From Damascus we turned westward, and by the route of Ain Fijeh, Abilah and Baalbec, reached Beirût on the 6th of May. This was the last of the Prince's remarkable approaches to the great Eastern cities, and

[1] *Lectures on the History of the Jewish Church*, p. 532, (Am. ed.)
[2] Acts ix. 14.

demands special notice from its contrast to the entry into Damascus. The welcome from the Christian population — now swelled far beyond its original proportions by the immigration of the fugitives from Damascus — was very striking. The ever deepening and multiplying crowd — the women wrapped in their white sheets — monks, soldiers, beggars, mingling in the procession, — the Greek clergy standing by the roadside throwing up incense as the Prince passed, — boys hanging on the branches of the wayside trees, inevitably, from their posture and their eastern costume, recalling the story and the pictures of Zacchæus,— the dust thickening, till the whole scene was enveloped as if in a dense cloud, — this was " the day the like of which," as it was said at the time, " Beirût had never seen before." They marvelled much to see the Prince enter in his simple travelling costume, without a crown on his head, or even a white plume in his hat; but they consoled themselves with the thought, that, had he travelled in royal pomp, it would have been impossible for him to have seen anything.

From Beirût the Prince visited Tyre and Sidon [1] on the south, and the entrance of the Lycus or Dog River on the north.

When I had visited this spot in 1853, the inscriptions and sculptures, which have made it so famous, had been very imperfectly deciphered. Since that time, the researches and the contests of scholars have fixed the attention of travellers on these curious memorials, here alone in the world united, of the three ancient Empires of

The Dog River.

[1] *See Sinai and Palestine,* c. vi.

Egypt, Assyria, and Rome — to which, in more modern times, have been added the marks of the early Empire of the Turks, and the present Empire of the French. These two more recent inscriptions may be briefly dismissed. The first, left by Selim I., the conqueror of Egypt and Palestine, is near the bridge which spans the river. The second was written to commemorate the occupation of Syria by the French army in 1860.[1] But those of the three former Empires are of permanent interest, the more so as their gradual resuscitation from the neglect of centuries has kept pace with the gradual advance of a more critical knowledge of the ancient world; and they have thus become, as it were, water-marks of its rising tide. The first that attracted the attention of modern travellers was the Latin inscription of the Emperor Antoninus to commemorate the cutting of the Roman road through the pass. This, which remained unobserved through the Middle Ages, was not beyond the comprehension of the travellers of the 17th and 18th centuries; and they accordingly have all noted and copied it. But the others, which have within the last few years riveted the regards of Europe, were then hardly thought worth a passing remark. Maundeville imagined them to be "perhaps the representations of some persons buried hereabouts." Pococke saw in them only "some small figures of men in relief . . . . very much de-

---

[1] It has sometimes been said that the French army erased one of the ancient inscriptions in order to substitute their own. This is not the case. The tablet on which their inscription (questionable, perhaps, under any circumstances) is written, though ancient, was blank. It is the one marked by Dr. Robinson (*Lat. Res.* p. 619), who saw it in 1852, as "No. 1, square at top; no figure, apparently no sculpture."

faced by time."[1] The Egyptian scholars first demanded for them the celebrity which they have since acquired. M. De Saulcy afterwards denied that any were Egyptian, and claimed them all for Assyria. It is now certain that of the nine tablets three are Egyptian, and six Assyrian; although it may be argued further [2] that Egyptian tablets have been, in some instances, appropriated by the Assyrian invaders six centuries afterwards, as one, at least, has been appropriated by the French invaders nearly three thousand years afterwards.

It is on these tablets alternating along the face of the cliff upon the ancient road, that the interest of the Biblical student is chiefly fixed.

There, side by side, we encounter the figures of the earliest and latest oppressors of Israel, — Rameses and Sennacherib.[3] Rameses must have passed by that road at a time when the course of Sacred history had hardly penetrated into Syria. His memorials can scarcely seem more ancient to us than they did to the first Grecian travellers who saw and recorded these or like vestiges of his conquests. When we trace the well-known figures — exactly as we see them on the temples of Thebes [4] — the King and the God, as usual, giving and receiving offerings — it is with much the

[1] See Robinson, *Lat. Res.* p. 623.
[2] *Ibid.* 622.
[3] See *Lectures on the History of the Jewish Church*, p. 100, (Am. ed.)
[4] The Egyptian sculptures are less distinct than the Assyrian. But the figures are unmistakably Egyptian; and though, as I saw them, it was difficult to conceive how Dr. Lepsius could have read the hieroglyphics, yet it was equally difficult to conceive how Dr. Robinson (p. 620) and others should have failed to see the figures. The fact is that, as he himself suggests, "under different conditions of light and shade," both sculptures and inscriptions become more or less visible or invisible.

same sense of remote antiquity as that with which Herodotus (if so be) must have climbed the same pathway, and "in the part of Syria called Palestine"[1] (to use his own words), "himself saw the monuments of Sesostris still in existence."

But the Assyrian tablets, if they do indeed contain the name, as they undoubtedly represent the country and empire, of *Sennacherib*, have a still more striking connection with the ancient history of Israel and of Syria. In the speech which is reported as delivered by his messenger in the historical narrative of the Prophet Isaiah,[2] the King of Assyria thus describes his march into Palestine :— "By the multitude of my chariots am I come up to the height of the mountains, to the 'edge' of Lebanon; and I have cut down the height of his cedars and the beauty of his fir-trees; and I entered into the height of his border, and the forest of his 'park.'" "I have digged and drunk water;" "I have made a 'bridge.'"[3]

"The multitude of his chariots," such as they are seen on the Assyrian monuments of the farther east, must have wound their difficult way through these romantic passes, up to the very "heights of the mountain" ranges, and along "the extreme edges of Leba-

---

[1] Herod. ii. 106. The word which Herodotus uses is στῆλαι. But this is frequently applied to slabs or tablets, as well as to pillars; and there can thus be but little doubt that these are the monuments which he professes to have seen. When we combine this fact with the frequent representations of a king bearing the same name (even although that name may be wrongly read), on the Egyptian temples, in connection with acts of conquest and triumph, we may safely argue (in contradiction to recent doubts), that there is a solid foundation for the history of a great Egyptian conqueror, whose arms extended as least as far as Syria.
[2] Isa. xxxvii. 24, 25.
[3] ἔθηκα γεφύραν. Isa. xxxvii. 25.

non," — along the banks of the streams which he drained off by his armies, or over which he threw bridges for them to pass. But there was one spot more sacred than all, to which the conqueror boasts that he had penetrated. He had gone into "the extremest height of Lebanon, the forest of its park:" and there he had cut down with ruthless insolence "the height of its cedars, the beauty of its fir-trees." [1]

These words may well be taken as an introduction to the next scene to which the course of our journey led us. We can hardly fail to see their application, if not to the actual grove of the present Cedars of Lebanon, at any rate to spots so like it, that the description of the one may justly be regarded as the description of the other. *The Cedars.*

Often as the Cedars have been seen, yet, as in the case of the first view of Niagara, or the first view of Jerusalem, an interest attaches to each new impression formed by every traveller who for the first time approaches them. In 1853 I had been prevented from visiting them by the snow which at that early season rendered them inaccessible, and on the present occasion the same obstacle shut us out from the usual route over the crest of the mountain from Baalbec, or even over its western shoulder by Afka. For this reason we approached the place from Tripoli. As the valley of Hasbeya is the sacred country of the Druzes, so the valleys and hills between Tripoli and Ehden, converging towards the deep glen of the "Holy River," the Kadisha, — probably so called from its numerous mon-

---

[1] I have left this rendering of the word in the English version unchanged. It may, however, be "cypresses" or "pines," or, perhaps even "young cedars."

asteries, — form the *Kesrouan*, the sacred country of the Maronites, the fierce Christian sect with which the Druzes are at deadly war. On the edge of the river is Kanobin (*Cœnobium*), the residence of their Patriarch. On the heights above is their chief village Ehden. It is from this village that the ascent is made to the Cedars.

A wide view opens of the long terraces of the Moraines[1] (to use the technical name) of ancient glaciers descending into the valley. A green slip of cultivated land reaches up into the verge of their desolate fields. Behind them is a semicircle of the snowy range of the summit of Lebanon. Just in the centre of the view, — in the dip between the Moraines and the snow-clad hills beyond, — is a single dark massive clump, the sole spot of vegetation that marks the mountain wilderness. This is the Cedar grove. It disappears as we ascend the intervening range, and does not again present itself till we are close upon it. Then the exactness of the Prophetic description comes out. It is literally on the very " edge " of the height of Lebanon, a " park " or " garden " of the forest; as truly as the " Jardin " or " garden " well known to Swiss travellers in the bosom of Mont Blanc. It is indeed worthy, from its mysterious elevation and seclusion, to be ranked by the Prophet Ezekiel as the " Garden of God."[2] It

---

[1] See J. H. Hooker, M. D., on the Cedars of Lebanon, *Nat. Hist. Rev.* v. 12, which contains the most complete scientific account of the cedars.

[2] Ezek. xxxi. 8, 9. "The Cedars in the Garden of God . . . all the trees of Eden that were in the Garden of God envied him." Gesenius interprets Eden here of the actual village, often mentioned in these pages, *Ehden*. It is said by Arabic scholars, that the difference of orthography is too great to admit of this identification. But the comparison of the Cedar Grove to the " Garden of God " remains unshaken.

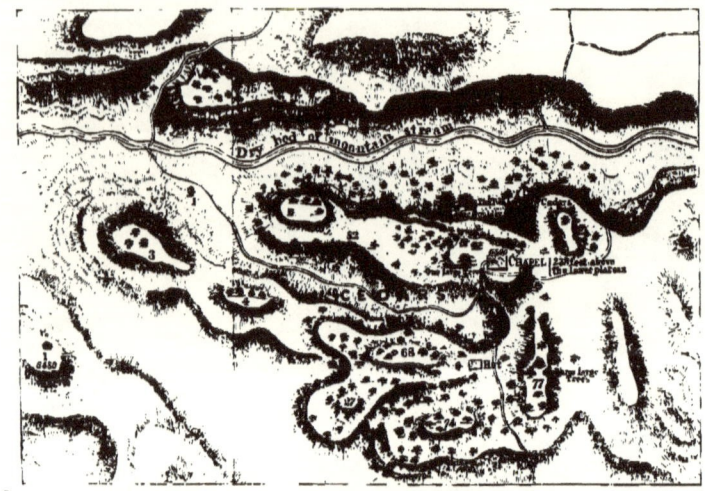

PLAN OF THE CEDARS OF LEBANON, AS SURVEYED BY COMMANDER A. L. MANSELL, R.N.
(*Published by permission of* ADMIRAL WASHINGTON, R. N.)
The figures in print indicate the number of trees in each group: the figures in italics, the height in feet above the level of the sea

IV.]   *THE CEDARS.*   253

stands as if on an island eminence, broken into seven [1] knolls, of which six are arranged round the seventh, a square mount in the midst of which stands a rude Maronite chapel. This variation of level and outline makes the whole group a kind of epitome of forest scenery. The outskirts of the eminence are clothed with the younger trees, whose light feathery branches veil the more venerable patriarchs in the interior of the grove. This younger growth, which has entirely sprung [2] up within the last two centuries, amounts now to more than three hundred. The older trees, which are so different in appearance from the others as to seem to belong to a different race, are now about twelve in number. Their forms are such as must always have impressed the imagination of those who saw them. Their massive trunks, clothed with a scaly texture, almost like the skin of living animals, and contorted with all the multiform irregularities of age, may well have suggested those ideas of regal, almost divine, strength and solidity which the Sacred Writers ascribe to them. They stand at the apex, so to say, of the vegetable world. "From the Cedar tree that is in Lebanon" downwards extends the knowledge of Solomon.[3] "To the Cedars of Lebanon" upwards reaches the destruction of the trees from the burning bramble of Jotham.[4] The intermarriage of the inferior plants [5] with the Cedar is the most inconceivable of all pre-

---

[1] Dr. Hooker mentions nine (*Nat. Hist. Rev.* v. 13), and this is the number brought out in the accompanying map, engraved by permission of Admiral Washington from the survey of Captain Mansell, R. N., of The Firefly. The variation is occasioned by reckoning within the circle two outlying hillocks.

[2] Dr. Hooker, p. 13.   [4] Judges ix. 15.
[3] 1 Kings iv. 33.   [5] 2 Kings xiv. 9.

sumption. The shivering of their rock-like stems[1] by the thunderbolt is like the shaking of the solid mountain itself.

In ancient days the grove must have been much more extensive, or rather, perhaps, the great trees then overspread the whole. Now they are huddled together on two or three of the central knolls, and the peculiar grace of the Cedar, as we see it in Europe, with its long sweeping branches, feathering down to the ground, is there unknown. In one or two instances the boughs of these aged trees are held up by a younger tree; others again of the smaller ones, whose trunks are decayed, are actually supported in the gigantic arms of their elder brethren. But in earlier times the breadth and extent of the trees seems to be as much noticed as their height and solidity. The Cedar is the model of the "spreading abroad"[2] — the constant "growth" of the righteous man; his boughs are "multiplied," and "become long," "fair," "thick,' "overshadowing"[3] in "length" and in "multitude." So vigorous and vast was the ancient life of the Cedars that it seemed as if all the snows and waters of Lebanon were gathered up into them. They are "filled," their "root is by great waters;" "the waters" make them great, "the deep sets them up on high."[4]

The spot thus becomes a centre to all the various

---

[1] Ps. xxix. 5.   [2] Ps. xlii. 13.
[3] Ezek. xxx. 3, 5, 7, 8.
[4] Ezek. xxxi. 4, 5, 7. "The rills from the surrounding heights collect on the upper flat and form one stream, which winds among the Moraines on its way to the lower flat, whence it is precipitated into the gorge of the Kadisha. The cedars grow on that portion of the Moraine which immediately borders this stream, and nowhere else." — *Dr. Hooker*, p. 12.

forms of the life of the wilderness in the midst of which it stands. "Nature was never silent in the forest; the cicale here were extraordinarily loud; and the trees were full of little birds of the brightest green and gold plumage, with a sweet clear note."[1] This is the scene which Ezekiel contemplates when he describes how under the Cedars "all the fowls of the air nestle, and all the beasts of the field bring forth their young."[2] Still more exactly it is the theatre in which the Psalmist gathers together the whole of animal life round "the Cedars which the Lord has planted;" "the birds making their nests," the "storks in the fir-trees," the marmot or *shaphan*[3] ("coney") in the surrounding cliffs; the chamois on the hills, the roaring of the lions in the stillness of the night[4] — whilst the distant view is filled up on the one side by the sea, with its monsters, its swarms of living creatures, and its ships;[5] and on the other by the "garment of light" in the sky, the "clouds" and "the wind" on the mountain; the "springs of the Kadisha and of the other rushing streams of the Lebanon; the cornfields and the vineyards on the nearer slopes for the service of humanity, — "to make glad and to strengthen the heart of man."

And if their very appearance and aspect thus connects them with the poetry of the Bible, their history

[1] Miss Beaufort's *Syrian Shrines*, 288. I quote from this as a detailed description of the Cedars in summer.
[2] Ezek. xxxi. 6.
[3] Ps. civ. 17, 18.
[4] Ps. civ. 21. Lions no longer exist in the Lebanon. But leopards, which also infested it formerly (Cant. iv. 8), are still found.
[5] Ps. civ. 25, 26. I owe this remark to a friend, who observed on the spot that all the natural features of the 104th Psalm are within view from the Cedars.

is also bound up with its history. We know not who first attacked the Cedars of Lebanon, but already in the time of David they were invaded for the building of the palaces at Jerusalem.[1] Many were the trees dragged down the steep descent, no doubt, to the harbor of Tripoli, to be embarked on rafts for Joppa. Thence they reappear in the woodwork of Solomon's Temple,[2] and in the vast palace, which from its rustic casing in cedar wood seemed to be almost a transplantation of the sacred grove to Jerusalem, " the house of the forest of Lebanon;"[3] whilst in the gardens the costly cedars, transplanted from Lebanon, seemed to have taken the place of the native sycamore.

For statues, for houses,[4] for masts of ships, the huge branches were carried off to Tyre and Zidon. But the great destroyer long remembered was Sennacherib. He, as we have seen, is described as making it his especial boast that he had penetrated to the sacred garden or park, and cut them down. It is on his approach probably that the Prophet's wail is lifted up, " Open thy doors, O Lebanon, that the fire may devour thy Cedars; howl, fir-tree, for the Cedar is fallen."[5] And in like manner, on his fall, the triumphant cry is raised in the lower world, " Yea, the fir-trees rejoice at thee and the Cedars of Lebanon, saying, since thou art laid down no feller is come up against us."[6] From that time they have become rarer and rarer. Other groups,

---

[1] 2 Sam. v. 11; vii. 2; 1 Chron. xxii. 4.
[2] 1 Kings v. 6, 8, 9; vi. 9, 10.
[3] 1 Kings vii. 2; x. 17, 27.
[4] See the passages quoted in Robinson's *Lat. Res.* 592.
[5] Zech. xi. 1, 2. It must be borne in mind that this passage probably belongs to the earlier prophet of that name. Zech. ix.-xiii.
[6] Isa. xiv. 8.

indeed, are said to exist in different parts of the mountain, but they have been seen only by two travellers.[1] By the sixth century the supply of cedar wood was almost, by the fifteenth century entirely, exhausted for the purposes of building. And now, for at least two centuries, they have become invested, by the veneration of pilgrims and by the increased admiration felt for natural objects, with a sanctity almost approaching to that with which they were formerly revered as special miracles of Divine power by the Psalmists of Israel. The old Hebrew name of *Arz* has never deserted them, and is even perpetuated in the puny imitation of them in the Western *Larch*.[2] The Maronites long guarded them, under penalties of excommunication:[3] they still honor them as the "Twelve Apostles," "the Friends of Solomon." The sanctuary, which was a rude altar, and is now a rude wooden chapel, they yearly frequent on the festival which the Oriental Church treats as the Feast of all "high mountains," the Feast of the Transfiguration.[4]

This was our last expedition in Syria. It was undertaken amidst storm and rain, which drove us from the Cedar grove, shortly after we had reached it, back to our encampment at Ehden. The bells of the Maronite churches — an unwonted, indeed an impossible, sound in any other region of Syria — (for they are tolerated nowhere else) were ringing, almost as if

---

[1] Robinson, *Lat. Res.* 592. Dr. Hooker (12) gives several reasons for doubting the ancient extent of the cedar forests.
[2] El-Arz, corrupted into *Alerce, Larch*.
[3] Robinson, *Lat. Res.* 590.
[4] On this day, the monks of Athos ascend the highest peak of that mountain, and celebrate a midnight service. See a striking description of it in *Vacation Tourists of* 1861, p. 118.

with the feeling of a European Sunday, as we re-entered the village. Close by our encampment stood the large deserted house — it might almost be called castle — of the Maronite chief Sheik Joseph, who, in consequence of some complications arising out of the late disturbances, had been banished to Constantinople. It was touching to see the excitement and distress of the villagers over the loss of their chief. Wherever we went — especially whenever the Prince appeared — there was the same cry amongst the men, the same beating of breasts and wailing amongst the women, " Restore us our Bey," Oh! restore us our Bey." It was after a walk through the village — in which we visited several of the churches and cottages of the place — that we found the stairs and corridors of the castle lined with a crowd of eager applicants, " sick people taken with divers diseases,"[1] who, hearing that there was a medical man in the party, had thronged round him, " beseeching him that he would heal them." I mention this incident because it illustrates so forcibly those scenes in the Gospel history, from which I have almost of necessity borrowed the language best fitted to describe the eagerness, the hope, the variety, of the multitude who had been attracted by the fame of this beneficent influence. It was an affecting scene; our kind Doctor was distressed to find how many cases there were which, with proper medical appliances, might have been cured; and, on returning to the ship, by the Prince's desire a store of medicines were sent back, with Arabic labels directing how, and for what purposes, they should be used.

On the 13th of May we left the shores of Syria,

[1] Matt. iv. 24; Luke vii. 3.

visiting only one more spot in departing; a spot rarely seen, but full of interest in connection both with Phœnicia and with the Cedars of Lebanon. Just where Lebanon, with its white line of snow, ends and melts away on the north into a range of low green hills, Phœnicia, and the last remains of Phœnicia, also end in the northernmost of the Phœnician cities, *Arvad*, *Aruad*, by the Greeks called *Aradus*, and now *Ruad*. Like Tyre, it was planted on a rocky island, a few miles from the shore; like Tyre, it is described by Strabo as crowded to excess by reason of the limited range of the island. In both cities this led to an arrangement which must have made them striking exceptions to most ancient, and to most Oriental, towns. For the sake of economizing the narrow space, the houses of both were built up, regardless of earthquakes, to the height of many stories, resembling the aspect of no other city of the old world,[1] except that of the gigantic mansions of Augustan Rome. These have all vanished; but on the western and north-western side of the island huge remnants still exist of the old wall, compacted of immense stones, and guarded by a vast trench cut through the living rock. M. Renan had, previously to my journey, represented these remains to me as the oldest of all the monuments of Syria; and such, from their massive, archaic appearance, they may well be supposed to be.

The Aradians or Arvadites were of old famous for their nautical skill, and are said to be so still. They

---

[1] Strabo, xvi. 753. It is a minute and characteristic proof of Lord Macaulay's extensive learning, that this feature of Tyre thus incidentally noticed by Strabo, is caught in the short passing notice of it in his History of England, vol. v. 204.

were selected from the rest of the Phœnicians for passing on rafts up and down the Lycus and up and down the Jordan;[1] probably in connection with the transport of the cedar wood to Jerusalem. If ever Syria were to recover anything of its former commercial position, the harbor of Ruad is said to be one of the best along its coast;[2] and in that case its inhabitants would regain some portion of their fame in ancient days, when they so powerfully contributed to the naval and military strength of Tyre :

> " High on the stately wall
> ' The spear of Arvad hung.' "

"The inhabitants of Arvad were thy mariners: the men of Arvad with thine army were upon thy walls round about."[3]

[1] Strabo xvi. 755.   [2] See Allen's *Dead Sea*, ii. 178.
[3] Ezek. xxvii. 8, 11. For a complete description of Ruad or Arvad, see Ritter's *Phœnicia and Lebanon*, p. 868-879.

PATMOS.

V. PATMOS.

THE island of Patmos does not fall within the course of any Mediterranean steamer. It was therefore only the opportunity afforded by our homeward voyage in H. M. Yacht Osborne, that enabled us to visit this sacred spot. We had already visited Rhodes and seen the excavation of one of the tombs at Camirus. We then passed through the marvellous crater of the ancient Thera, the modern Santorin, and landed on the almost desert island of Antiparos, to explore its famous grotto, and, early on the morning of the 17th of May, reached the harbor of Patmos.

It is one of those spots of which there are not a few in the world, — especially in connection with Sacred History, — which present an entire blank for centuries, and then by one single incident acquire an absolutely universal celebrity. Such in Palestine are Nazareth and Capernaum, unknown in the long period of Jewish history till they became the homes of Christ. Such in the Mediterranean are Malta and Patmos.

Malta, after years of obscurity, suddenly springs into light, when S. Paul and his companions landed on its shores from the driving storm and "knew that the island was called Melita."[1] This, indeed, was but the beginning of its fame. A modern history was still in

[1] Acts xxvii. 1.

reserve for it, when fifteen centuries afterwards it became the refuge of the Knights of S. John, and after three centuries yet again, the fortress of the English power in the Mediterranean.

But Patmos owes its fame solely to its connection with "the Revelation of S. John the Divine."[1] Before that time it is mentioned but three times in the whole course of classical literature; twice in the merely passing notices of Strabo and Pliny; once in relation to Greek history, when the Athenian general Paches pursued the Lacedemonian fleet "as far as Patmos."[2]

An inscription, preserved in the island, seems to show that its original name was *Patnos;* and this, like many other archaisms of the Greek language, has been perpetuated in the common dialect of the country, in which it is still called *Patino*.[3] A legend derived the name from πάτημα "the footstep" or "stepping-stone" of the Sea God. The Italian corruption of *Palmosa* probably arose from the palms, which, with the rest of the vegetation of the island, have gradually disappeared, and now only are to be found in one spot called "the Saint's Garden."

The island is about fifteen miles in circumference. It is remarkable from the complexity of its shape and outline; in this respect bearing a singular resemblance to Ithaca, and presenting a striking example of that indentation and variety of coast, which has been often

---

[1] I do not here enter into any of the other questions connected with the Apocalypse. But its association with Patmos is undoubted.

[2] Strabo x. p. 488; Pliny iv. 23; Thucyd. iii. 23.

[3] See *Description de l'Ile de Patmos*, par V. Guerin. Paris, 1856. From this work (the knowledge of which I owe to the kindness of my friend Dr. Howson) I have taken the account of the classical notices of the island, and of the legendary life of S. John, by his disciple Prochorus.

remarked as characteristic of European, and, above all, of Grecian geography. Small as it is, Patmos is broken asunder into two separate insulated peaks, united only by a narrow isthmus, and whilst the rocky hills are broken into innumerable crags, the shore is indented with innumerable bays. The original capital was apparently where the little seaport town (La Scala) now stands in the creek formed by the isthmus. Its ancient name seems to have been Phora, and its Acropolis stood on a rocky hill immediately behind. The present city (so to call it) is clustered round the monastery of S. John, on the summit of the southernmost of the two peaks of which the island is composed. This change of situation is worth noticing as an illustration of two characteristics of ancient historical topography; the first, that which Thucydides[1] has noticed in Greece generally; the removal of the town inland from its original situation, where it was more exposed to the attacks of pirates, — a calamity to which the secluded situation, and at the same time the accessible bays, of Patmos rendered it singularly liable; the second, that which I have already noticed in speaking of Hebron, — the tendency of the population to desert their old secular habitations, for the sake of clustering round the new spots, less convenient for intercourse, but more available for the sacred resort of pilgrims and worshippers.[2]

" I John was," or rather " became a dweller,"[3] " in the isle that is called Patmos for the word of God and

[1] Thucyd. i. 7.
[2] The monastery was founded by a rich Greek, Christodulos, in 1070. This contains the celebrated Library, and the Charter of the Foundation granted by Alexius Comnenus.
[3] See Dr. Wordsworth on Rev. i. 9. ἐγενόμην not ἦν.

for the testimony of Jesus Christ." This is the sum total of our authentic information of the circumstances of S. John's stay in Patmos. But it agrees with the general tradition of the early Christian writers that, whether under Nero or Domitian, he was exiled thither. That Patmos should have been selected as a place of exile is in conformity with the general usage of the Roman Empire, according to which the islands of the Mediterranean were employed for this purpose; and the curious simplicity of the explanation, "an isle *that is called* Patmos," agrees with the actual seclusion, and (as before noticed) the previous obscurity, of the Island itself.

The connection of Patmos with this famous exile divides itself into two parts: that which is legendary or traditional, and that which directly illustrates the Book of the Apocalypse.

(1.) The traditional details are contained in a work Traditions. called " The Travels of S. John in Patmos," professing to be written by his disciple Prochorus, and accepted by the Greek Church as authentic. It is evidently a late work, consisting chiefly of prodigies performed by S. John, and particularly of a contention with a demon of the name of Cynops, who lived at the southern extremity of the island, and was ultimately transformed (as in the corresponding legends of the Odyssey at Corcyra) into a rock, still shown in the harbor. Historically worthless as is this story, it is interesting as the only record of the ancient names of the villages of the island. It is also remarkable from its omissions. It contains no allusion to the Latin legend of S. John's Roman persecution; and it has no mention of the Apocalypse. It would seem as if the ecclesiastical jealousy which so long prevented the recognition of the Apocalypse amongst the Canonical Scriptures, had thrown it into the shade even in the legends of Patmos.

On the composition of the Gospel, however, the legend lays much stress; and this it places, not, according to the usual and probable tradition, at Ephesus, but in Patmos. In a striking passage, which rises above the flatness of the rest of the narrative, the Apostle is described as found by his disciple standing wrapt in prayer. He bids Prochorus take pen and paper; a flash of lightning and a peal of thunder shake the rocky mountain, and the Apostle bursts forth, "In the beginning of the Word," and so, he standing and Prochorus seated at his feet, the Gospel is recited by him from first to last. The scene of this transaction is laid by the legend at a spot called "The Repose" (κατάπαυσις). This is still pointed out, and is, in fact, the only locality in the island directly connected by tradition with the Apostle's visit. It is a small chapel half-way up the hill, between the town on the summit and the port at the foot. It professes to be built over the cave, in which the vision of the Apocalypse was seen, and the commencement of the Gospel was written. The rocky floor and rocky roof of the cave are visible in one of the side chapels. Of the Apocalypse the record is merely a picture on the Iconostasis of the inner chapel, representing the vision of the Angels of the Seven Churches, and S. John asleep beneath. As in the legendary biography, the composition of the Gospel takes the chief place. S. John appears in a picture dictating it to Prochorus, under the light of an illuminating ray; at the entrance is shown the exact spot where he pronounced the opening sentence of the Prologue; and a triple fissure appears in the roof, through which, according to the barbarous simplicity of the legend, the doctrine of the Trinity is said to have been revealed to him.

(2.) But the real interest of a visit to Patmos consists, not in the endeavor to ascertain these special localities of a doubtful tradition, which, even if true, would throw no clear light on the events or characters in question, but in the inquiry how far the general situation yields any illustration of the vision of which it is the scene.

Illustrations of the Apocalypse.

The Discourses of the Gospels and the Epistles of S. Paul are raised, for the most part, too far above the local circumstances of their time, to allow of more than a very slight contact with the surrounding scenery. It is only when the teaching assumes a more directly pictorial or poetic form, as in the Parables of the Gospels, or the Athenian speech of S. Paul, that the adjacent imagery can be expected to bear its part. But this is precisely what we might expect to find in the Apocalypse. The "Revelation" is of the same nature as the prophetic visions and lyrical psalms of the Old Testament, where the mountains, valleys, trees, storms, earthquakes, of Palestine occupy the foreground of the picture, of which the horizon extends to the unseen world and the remote future.

For this reason I had always eagerly desired to visit the island of Patmos. I was not disappointed. The stern rugged barrenness of its broken promontories well suits the historical fact of the relegation of the condemned Christian to its shores, as of a convict to his prison. And the view from its summit, with the general character of its scenery, still more deeply enters into the figures of the vision itself.

He stood on the heights of Patmos in the centre of a world of his own. The island, then probably less inhabited than now, was almost a solitude. "He was in the Spirit," withdrawn from earthly things, like Moses on Sinai, or Elijah on Carmel. But the view from the topmost peak, or, indeed, from any lofty elevation in the island, unfolds an unusual sweep, such as well became the "Apocalypse," the "*unveiling*" of the future to the eyes of the solitary seer. It was "a great and high mountain,"[1] whence he could see things to come. Above, there was always the broad heaven of a Grecian sky; sometimes bright, with its "white cloud,"[2] sometimes torn with "lightnings and thunderings," and darkened[3] by "great hail," or cheered with "a rainbow like unto an emerald." Over the high tops of Icaria, Samos, and Naxos rise the mountains of Asia Minor; amongst which would lie, to the north, the circle of the Seven Churches to which his addresses were to be sent. Around him stood the mountains and islands of the Archipelago, — "every mountain and *island*[4] shall be moved out of their places;" "every *island* fled away, and the *mountains*[5] were not found." At his feet lay Patmos itself, like a huge serpent, its rocks contorted into the most fantastic and grotesque forms, which may well have suggested the "beasts" with many heads and monstrous figures,[6] the "huge dragon," struggling for victory, — a connection as obvious as that which has

[1] Rev. xxi. 10.
[2] *Ibid.* xiv. 14.
[3] *Ibid.* iv. 3; viii. 7; xi. 19; xvi. 21.
[4] *Ibid.* vi. 14.
[5] *Ibid.* xii. 3, 9; xvi. 20.
[6] *Ibid.* xiii. 1, 21; xvii. 3.

often been recognized between the strange shapes on the Assyrian monuments and the prophetic symbols in the visions of Ezekiel and Daniel. When he stood "on the sand of the sea,"[1] the sandy beach at the foot of the hill, he would see these strange shapes "rise out of the sea"[2] which rolled before him. When he looked around, above or below, "the *sea*" would always occupy the foremost place. He saw "the things that are in the heavens and in the earth and *in the sea*."[3] The angel was "not to hurt the earth or the *sea*,"[4] nor "to blow on the earth or *on the sea*." "A great mountain," like that of the volcanic Thera, "as it were burning with fire," was "to be cast into *the sea*."[5] The angel was to stand with "his right foot *upon the sea*,[6] and his left foot on the earth;" "the vial was to be poured out *upon the sea;*"[7] the voices of heaven were like the sound of the waves beating on the shore, as "the sound of many waters;"[8] "the millstone was cast *into the sea;*"[9] "the *sea* was to give up the dead which were in it;"[10] and the time would come when this wall of his imprisonment, which girdled round the desolate island, should have ceased; "there shall be no more *sea*."[11]

Such was the scene of the Apocalypse, varied, doubtless, by other images drawn from the Prophetic books of the older Scriptures, and from the report or the

---

[1] Rev. xiii. 1.
[2] Ibid. xiii. ii.
[3] Ibid. v. 13; x. 6; xiv. 7.
[4] Ibid. vii. 1–3.
[5] Ibid. viii. 8. I have not enlarged upon this. But the extraordinary aspect of Thera (the modern Santorin), even when its volcanic fires were dormant, may well have furnished this image.
[6] Rev. x. 2, 5, 8.
[7] Ibid. xvi. 3.
[8] Ibid. xiv. 2; xix. 6.
[9] Ibid. xviii. 21.
[10] Ibid. xx. 13.
[11] Ibid. xxi. 1.

actual sight of the great cities of the earth. These peculiarly local illustrations, be they many or few, of the Apocalyptic Vision contrast remarkably with the total absence of illustration of the Gospel and Epistles of S. John as derived from the sight of Ephesus. The ruins of Ephesus we saw on the evening of the same day. The remains of the theatre, built into the side of Mount Pion,[1] if we people it once again with its furious mob, piled tier above tier, in the face of their beloved temple of Diana, give a lively picture of the outbreak of the Ephesian silversmiths against S. Paul.[2] But there is nothing to recall S. John, except the rock-hewn tomb, called by his name, near the summit of the deserted hill. The grave of the greatest of all the Apostles, — if we may measure greatness by the divine excellence of the works which bear his name, — lies overgrown with brushwood, and only marked by the broken offerings of a few Greek peasants. It is, if we choose so to view it, a true emblem of the spiritual elevation of his spirit and of his words above any mere earthly associations of time or place. We understand the Apocalypse better for having seen Patmos. But we can understand the Gospel and Epistles of S. John as well in England as in Patmos or Ephesus, or even in his own native Palestine.

Ephesus.

It is needless to follow the homeward route, through the well-known scenes of Smyrna, Constantinople,

[1] This seems to be the correct orthography of the hill usually called Prion. See Faulkner's *Ephesus*, p. 27.
[2] Acts xix. 29.

Athens, Cephallonia, and Malta, to the conclusion of our Eastern Tour in the harbor of Marseilles. A rapid journey brought us through France. On the evening of the 14th of June, His Royal Highness reached Windsor Castle; and the travellers, who had lived together in unbroken intercourse for more than four eventful months, parted to their several homes. From one, — the chief of our expedition, — it was a parting for life. General Bruce on the 27th of June, within a fortnight after our return, sank under the effects of a fever contracted during his journey in the East. To him, the Queen and the lamented Prince had confided the anxious charge of the Eastern Tour. Through his unwearied exertions it was brought to its prosperous conclusion; and, if in the foregoing pages it has appeared that any fresh instruction or profit was gained from revisiting these sacred scenes, this valued increase of knowledge is an additional ground for always recalling with gratitude the memory of his thoughtful care, as well as the kindness and consideration, from the highest to the humblest, of all those who cheered the trials and shared the pleasures of our travels in the East.

www.ingramcontent.com/pod-product-compliance
Lightning Source LLC
Chambersburg PA
CBHW031934230426
43672CB00010B/1919